MW00992566

Recruiting and Hiring Effective Teachers:

A Behavior-Based Approach

Mary C. Clement

Because research and information make the difference.

E R S

Educational Research Service
1001 North Fairfax Street, Suite 500 • Alexandria, VA 22314-1587
Phone: 703-243-2100 • Toll Free: 800-791-9308
Fax: 703-243-1985 • Toll Free: 800-791-9309
Email: ers@ers.org • Web site: www.ers.org

Educational Research Service is the nonprofit organization serving the research and information needs of the nation's preK-12 education leaders and the public. Founded by the national school management associations, ERS provides quality, objective research and information that enable education leaders to make the most effective school decisions in both day-to-day operations and long-range planning. Refer to the end of this book for information on the benefits of an annual ERS subscription, and for an order form listing resources that complement this book. Or visit us online at www.ers.org for an overview of available resources.

ERS e-Knowledge Portal
http://portal.ers.org

ERS Founding Organizations:
American Association of School Administrators
American Association of School Personnel Administrators
Association of School Business Officials International
National Association of Elementary School Principals
National Association of Secondary School Principals
National School Public Relations Association

ERS Executive Staff:
Katherine A. Behrens, Acting President and Chief Operating Officer
Kathleen McLane, Chief Knowledge Officer

Copyright © 2008 Educational Research Service. All Rights Reserved.

Library of Congress Cataloging-in-Publication Data
Clement, Mary C.
  Recruiting and hiring effective teachers : a behavior-based approach / Mary C. Clement.
     p. cm.
  ISBN 978-1-931762-68-7
  1. Teachers—Recruiting—United States. 2. Teachers—Selection and appointment—United States. 3. Employment interviewing—United States—Psychological aspects. I. Title.
   LB2835.25.C543 2007
   331.7′61371100973—dc22   2007050524

Author: Mary C. Clement
Editor: Cheryl Bratten
Layout & Design: Joe Broderick and Libby McNulty

Ordering Information: Additional copies of this publication may be purchased at the base price of $30.00; ERS School District Subscriber: $15.00; ERS Individual Subscriber: $22.50. Quantity discounts available. Add the greater of $4.50 or 10% of total purchase price for shipping and handling. Phone orders accepted with Visa, MasterCard, or American Express. Stock No. 0709. ISBN 978-1-931762-68-7.

Note: ERS is solely responsible for this publication; no approval or endorsement by ERS founders is implied.

Contents

About the Author

 Mary C. Clement was a high school foreign language teacher before earning a doctorate in curriculum and instruction from the University of Illinois at Urbana-Champaign in 1991. She directed the beginning teacher program at Eastern Illinois for six years and is now an associate professor of teacher education at Berry College, northwest of Atlanta, GA. In addition to undergraduate courses in methods and management, she teaches graduate courses in curriculum theory and supervision and mentoring.

She is the author of *Building the Best Faculty, So You Want to Be a Teacher,* and *First Time in the High School Classroom*, from Scarecrow Education/Rowman & Littlefield Education, and *ABC's of Job-Hunting for Teachers*, from Kappa Delta Pi. Her articles have appeared in the *Kappan, Principal Leadership, The Clearing House*, and Kappa Delta Pi's *Educational Forum* and *Record*. She presents workshops for administrators on the topics of interviewing and hiring new teachers. She can be reached at drmaryclem@comcast.net or mclement@berry.edu.

Preface

"Increasingly, reports from research and practice may suggest that a teacher's hiring experience may influence her satisfaction and retention in teaching" (Johnson, Berg, & Donaldson, 2005, p. 28)

Over 25 years after my first job interview for a teaching position, I still remember exactly how it went. Some of the things that happened in my first interview were quite good—such as including another teacher in the process who could ask specifics about my ideas on the teaching of Spanish and French. Other things that came up in the interview probably didn't help the interviewer determine if I could actually do the job of teaching—since we talked about growing up on a farm, my year abroad in Spain, and my interest (or lack there of) in coaching! Times have indeed changed, and job interviews in all fields, including teaching, have become more professional and polished. In an attempt to be more efficient and scientific, interviewing has become a field of study with a knowledge base created by the generation of much literature. The shelf space for books about interviewing is quite extensive at most book stores, and career center directors and interview coaches stay busy teaching how to interview.

I first became aware of behavior-based interviewing (BBI) in 1999 when I read an article that a friend had written about it for a local business publication in Illinois (Kistner, 1999). The interviewing strategy of determining the skills and experiences needed to do a job, and then asking candidates about their past behaviors, opportunities, and successes with those skills, seemed to make perfect sense. I asked myself, "Are we doing this kind of interviewing to hire new teachers, and if not, why aren't we?"

Digging into the idea of applying BBI to teacher interviews, I have found very little written about it. Nagy (2002) wrote about behavioral interviewing for educators with regard to how new teachers should answer questions posed in this style. Harold P. Brull uses behavior-description interview questions when teaching his workshops about hiring teachers and other school personnel (Clement, Kistner, & Moran, 2005). Stronge and Hindman (2003) touch upon the premise of BBI when they write about "using the domains of teacher effectiveness to select candidates" (p. 50). Perhaps others have written, as well.

My own research about the use of BBI in teacher hiring indicates that the world of education has a long way to go before saying that this is the way we hire new teachers (Clement, 2002). Yet, as the need for new teachers increases, and as the need to be more efficient and effective in hiring quality teachers grows, the world of education may well want to look at BBI as its model.

Who Can Use This Book?

This book is written for all those involved in hiring new teachers. Personnel directors, superintendents, principals, department chairs, and teachers on hiring committees will find this a valuable tool for recruiting, interviewing, hiring, and retaining new teachers. The book is both a "how-to" and a reference to the most current research in the field. The history of BBI and the need for it are covered, as are the steps that are preliminary to actual interviewing. Much time is devoted to actual interview questions, and how to create a customized list for your school's needs. Very importantly, the assessment and evaluation of candidate answers is outlined with strategies for making your hiring decisions based on more than instincts and feelings. Teachers who are job searching could certainly hone their interview skills by reading this resource.

Chapter 1
The Need for Best Interviewing Practice

It seems that the hiring process used to be easier. In most areas, if a teacher retired, moved away, or left the profession, a principal could post the opening with three or four colleges and garner enough applications to find qualified people to interview. An interview consisted of getting to know the applicant, talking about student teaching or previous teaching, and trying to determine if the candidate would "fit in" to the community and stay in the position. Job interviews often began with the question, "Tell me about yourself" and ended with "What do you see yourself doing five to ten years down the road?" The candidates who got hired were from teacher education programs that the interviewer trusted, and who may have indicated family ties to the area.

Fast forward from the good old days of easier school staffing to today's challenges of recruiting and hiring highly qualified teachers. Widely publicized calls have been made for the hiring of "competent, caring, qualified" teachers (National Commission on Teaching and America's Future, 1996) and the federal mandate of No Child Left Behind (NCLB) further forced the issue of hiring fully qualified teachers.

In addition to the demand to hire the best, the need for new teachers is increasing. "In some regions, the demand for new teachers is already outpacing the supply" (Scherer, 1999, p. vii). As student enrollments grow, even more new teachers will be needed. According to Breaux and Wong (2003), "In the next ten years, America will need to hire two million new teachers to meet rising enrollment demands and replace an aging teaching force. Half of our nation's teachers will retire during this period" (p. 4). Debate exists about the nature of teacher shortages, and the problem of shortages may lie "…in the distribution of teachers" (Voke, 2003, p. 4). Urban and rural areas often experience shortages, while suburban districts continue to be flooded with applicants.

Hiring new teachers who are prepared to teach an increasingly diverse student body adds to the challenge of staffing schools (Futrell, Gomez, & Bedden, 2003). As special needs students and linguistically diverse student numbers increase, so does the need to hire more teachers who are equipped to teach special education and bilingual/ESL classes. Annual research from the American Association for Employment in Education (2004) indicates teacher shortages in many fields of special education, English as a second language, bilingual education, and Spanish, as well as in mathematics, sciences, and computer science/technology.

Staffing the schools of high-needs urban areas may have special challenges. Since his noted 1995 book, *Star Teachers of Children in Poverty*, Martin Haberman has worked to improve the hiring of teachers who will persist and succeed in urban schools. According to Haberman, an interview can make a difference in hiring a teacher who will succeed with at-risk children.

What the business world has referred to as employee turnover, the education profession views as a lack of retention, with low retention rates fueling teacher shortages. Retention issues may begin as early as college graduation, as Linda-Darling Hammond (2001) has written that "…only 60 to 70 percent of newly prepared teachers enter teaching jobs immediately after they graduate…" (p. 12). Once new teachers do enter the profession, many leave during the first 3 to 5 years (Haberman, 1995; Ingersoll & Smith, 2003). Some research suggests that even experienced teachers who are conscientious and well established may be leaving their jobs in higher numbers than in the past due to challenges of the profession (Tye & O'Brien, 2002).

In reality, "the fear of the teacher shortage, which is predicted to get worse over the next several years, pervades the profession" (Heller, 2004, p. 1). The need to constantly hire new teachers emanates from many sources: growing student enrollments, more special needs students, low teacher retention rates, teacher retirements, and shortages in certain geographic areas and subject matter fields. Ingersoll (2003) described the situation well, saying that, "The sheer size of the teaching force, combined with the relatively high annual turnover of the teaching occupation, means that there are relatively large flows into, through, and from schools each year. The image these data suggest is a revolving door" (p. 148). It is because of this revolving door that school administrators are faced with spending more and more time interviewing and hiring new teachers.

The Need for Efficient, Reliable Interviewing Techniques

"All good schools have one thing in common: good teachers. Top-quality teaching fosters high student achievement—and high achievers can harness their talents and energies and become successful, contributing citizens" (The Teaching Commission, 2004, p. 12).

Why should administrators spend time and effort in hiring? Simply put, good teachers do not grow on trees! Schools with high faculty turnover will quickly develop bad reputations, which will make it even harder to keep qualified teachers. Parent complaints may grow with high faculty turnover, further lessening community support. Building administrators know that their jobs are much easier when the faculty is working efficiently. Above all else, students deserve quality teachers—ones who are committed to best professional practices.

What makes a good employee? What makes a good teacher? Are there skills or experiences that make some individuals the best teachers, and if so, how do we determine that a candidate has attained the right skills and mastered the minimal experiences? In a perfect world, an administrator might have time to observe a candidate teach for two hours in a real classroom before inviting the individual for an interview. If technology were just a little more advanced, perhaps videos of candidates would give us more insight into teaching skills, or perhaps we could watch student teachers online as they delivered lessons to see if they really were ready for their first jobs. Portfolios, both electronic and paper, can provide insights into the candidate's experiences and his or her ability to reflect on those experiences, but reading the contents of a four-inch binder may take hours, even if it is compressed onto one disc. The real world gives us time and budget constraints, and the truth is that on-site interviewing will probably remain the most useful tool for determining which candidates receive job offers. While the interview has always been a tool for sorting and ranking the best candidates, it may now be viewed as an early step in recruiting the strongest candidates as well.

"First we need to look at our hiring practices. Effective recruiting needs to be seen as the first step in effective retention. Have we hired the right person for the job? Is the candidate qualified on paper? Will the candidate be motivated by what our job offers? Will the candidate demonstrate the success factors needed for the position? A company's recruiting, hiring, and orientation process can do much more than get the employee in the door. These processes can increase the propensity that the employee will stay around for a while" (Herrera, 2001, p. 87).

Why Behavior-Based Interviewing?

Behavior-based interviewing (BBI) is not new, at least not to the business world. Called behavior-description interviewing by Janz, Hellervik, and Gilmore (1986), they described it as follows:

> [It] is not a minor facelift for traditional interviewing techniques; it differs substantially from them. BD (behavior description) interviewing accuracy exceeds traditional interviewing accuracy by three to seven times, and that improved accuracy makes BD interviewing highly cost-effective. Finally, cream-of-the-crop applicants prefer BD interviews and are more willing to accept jobs with organizations that use them. In short, BD interviewing rewards, challenges, and excites, but it also demands hard work. (p. 3)

Now commonly known as behavior-based interviewing, this strategy is based on the premise that past behavior is the best predictor of future performance. Deems (1994) further explains:

> The single best predictor of a candidate's future job perfor-
> mance is his or her past job behavior. How do we know this
> is true? Because it's been proved [sic] in thousands of actual
> job situations for more than two decades. Interviews that
> probe for past job behavior have been found to be more
> reliable than ones that focus on personality traits, such as
> "I'm dependable," or "I'm hardworking," or even "You can
> count on me." And hiring decisions based on actual behav-
> ior are far more accurate than those based on gut feelings.
> (p. 9)

Green (1996) writes that jobs are evolving and that there are new
ways of working. He contends that,

> As the concept of the job has evolved, so has the interview.
> More and more attention is being paid to finding not just a
> likable person but a worker with a specific set of skills who
> can adapt as job requirements change. The result is an over-
> all trend toward a more scientific selection process (p. 23).

Bringing BBI into Teacher Interviews

Typically, a BBI question begins with a phrase such as "tell about a
time when…," "describe an example when you…," "what have you
done in the past to…," or "what have you implemented…." In the
business world, behavior-based questions might include:

- Tell us about a time when you worked in a group to design
  and finish a project.
- Describe how you have managed conflict when you and a co-
  worker had a disagreement.

- What strategies have you implemented to enhance customer satisfaction?
- Describe an assignment where you had leadership duties and how you organized the work to be done.
- Tell about a time when an assignment or project was not a success and how you reacted to that.
- Tell us about your experiences in creating and managing budgets.

In order to apply the strategy of BBI to teacher interviews, the employer will have to decide what specific skills and experiences are necessary to ensure success of the new hire in a particular school setting, and then ask about those experiences. If the interviewer feels that classroom management is a priority, then a set of questions should be asked about specific management issues. If the teaching of reading is a priority, then questions about reading strategies are asked. Each school has its own student demographics and unique school climate. Designing and asking questions geared to the candidate's experiences with similar schools and demographic populations may help the employer determine if the candidate has sufficient experience to thrive in this new setting. For example:

- Tell us how you have established a workable classroom management plan in the past.
- What have your experiences been teaching reading with the balanced approach?
- Describe a lesson that you taught that incorporated phonics.
- Describe your experiences working with high-needs students.
- Tell us about a success you have experienced with a single student or a class.

The amount of information that an employer can glean from just these five questions will provide much more insight into the candidate's skills than questions such as "Tell me about yourself," "Why do you want to be a teacher?", or "What was your school experience like as a student?"

When applied to teacher selection interviews, BBI calls upon the candidate to relate experiences in previous teaching, student teaching, or field experience. Some questions will require a student to articulate material learned in college classes, and then apply that material to a school setting. While it can be argued, for example, that being able to talk about classroom management is different than actually being able to manage a classroom of 12-year olds, it can also be defended that a candidate who can clearly state how he or she plans for management will be more able to begin managing a classroom on the first day of school.

The opposite is also defensible—that a candidate who cannot explain how to assign grades in a fifth-grade math classroom probably has not learned a system for grading and will have difficulty in this area without further training (Clement, 2004). Hence, BBI can help the interviewer sort the candidates who have had the training, know the pertinent skills, and can start teaching on day one. Teaching is certainly a unique job because a new hire must generally begin the first day with all the responsibilities of a veteran for the instruction, management, and assessment of the students in the room. Additionally, teachers are responsible for a myriad of ancillary duties, varying in degree from mitten-finding to child abuse reporting. A skilled teacher is truly a "good hire" for a school, and BBI should help to identify the best hires from the pool of applicants.

Chapter 2
The Recruitment Process

"A Harvard Business School study determined that more than 75 percent of turnover could be traced back to poor hiring practices. The leading contributor to turnover is often not what happens after the employee is hired, but rather the process leading up to it" (McKenna, 2004, p. 16).

Who Becomes a Teacher?

Anyone who has interviewed prospective teachers knows that at some time during the interview an elementary education major will say, "I just love working with children." Research indicates that the number one reason elementary education majors cite for entering the profession is love of children. Secondary majors cite their love of subject matter and middle grades majors may fall somewhere in between the other two reasons (Parkay & Stanford, 1998; Wiseman, Knight, & Cooner, 2002).

Rather than ignoring these obvious reasons, we need to capitalize on them. Recruit high school teachers from universities with strong subject-matter programs and let candidates know that they will spend their time teaching in their field, with extracurricular duties and out-of-field teaching being minimal, if at all. Recruit elementary majors from programs where a lot of emphasis is placed on working with children in every class, not just student teaching. Also, some elementary majors want only a certain grade, so matching candidates who want the grade where your opening exists is a good way to ensure the candidate will accept an offer and stay in the job.

Envisioning/Redefining Teaching Positions

At many schools, people become programs. A middle school may have a teacher who teaches English and offers exploratory German 2 hours a day on a rotating basis. A high school may have a veteran math teacher who excels at teaching AP calculus, AP physics, and one auto shop class a year. Some elementary teachers enjoy the opportunity to teach gifted sections or to be reading coaches as well as have their own classroom. It may not be wise to advertise for any of these positions as they now exist.

Rather, consider configuring those positions differently. The redefining of a middle-school position into two half-time jobs, or the high school position into one math job for vocational education and then the addition of AP physics to another science teacher's load may net a stronger pool of candidates. When a veteran teacher leaves, his or her ancillary duties may be accepted, even appreciated, by some other teachers who want a small change, then the new position can be outlined as one that more candidates would be qualified for and interested in. A strong candidate should ask, "Why is this position open?" Your answer can be a recruitment tool, if it indicates that the administration has put thought into this position so that it is a do-able one for a new hire.

How do we get around the age-old problem of giving the new hires the worst assignments? Recent graduates still report that in some schools the "newbies" have to prove their worth by working with the students that nobody else wants and that they have to work in the hottest/

coldest/smallest/worst classroom left. While it is hard to satisfy every faculty member, strong leadership is needed to make the first year a successful one. Some new teachers are used to being "A" students and not suffering any failures. An impossible teaching assignment the first year may lead them straight into a job in the insurance business! The old adage about breaking up the "trouble-makers" and making all classes heterogeneous may have some merit. Not allowing veteran teachers to hand-pick their students may be another solution. (Yes, this does go on in some elementary schools.) Perhaps the best answer is to be honest with the new hires about the position available from the start, to lower all class sizes for better teacher/student ratios, and to ensure that a new teacher has a lot of help from mentors, special education teachers, and administration for dealing with the given assignment.

Truth in Advertising

In the business world, recruiters provide job applicants with "realistic job previews" (RJPs) that "include both positive and negative aspects of the job" (Liu, 2005, p. 8). The premise behind the use of RJPs is that the more accurately the candidate perceives the position, the more likely his or her expectations will be met. "As a result, new employees are more likely to be satisfied with their jobs and less likely to leave voluntarily" (Liu, 2005, p. 9).

If there were complete truth in advertising, an advertisement for a new teacher might read something like this:

> **Wanted: Competent, Caring, and Qualified Teacher**
> Student–focused, passionate professional, committed to learning, and well versed in subject-area content. Understands

human development and learning, thrives on chaos, avoids burnout and withdrawal by remaining engaged in own learning. Leads successfully in technological milieu, arbitrates disputes, and juggles multiple tasks (Steffy, Wolfe, Pasch, & Enz, 2000, p. 1).

Basic truth in advertising means not leaving out important information or misleading a candidate. A first-year teacher once told me she was interviewed and hired to teach five general English classes. When she arrived at the large high school, the five classes were ones where all non-diagnosed special education students and class repeaters were grouped. It was a nightmare, especially considering that English was her minor and she had student taught with honors English and drama/journalism classes! Not a good match, and of course, the teacher would leave that position. With truth in advertising, this position should have been presented as one needing an applicant with English and special education background. Yes, there are candidates who want to teach these classes. In fact, an English teacher who was working on a master's in special education would have been a better hire, but finding that combination would have taken much more recruiting. Perhaps giving one of each of the classes to other teachers and creating a position that was four general English classes and one of these remedial classes would have been a better solution.

Another truth in advertising issue concerns student demographics. Most new graduates go online and learn about your school before they ever apply for a job there. If you are advertising regionally and nationally for hard-to-fill positions, be sure and include some information about student demographics. Again, honesty is the best policy. If a school is a "high priority" one with sagging test scores and low socio-economic factors, the only new hires who will strive to do their best and stay are the ones who know what to expect. There are some high needs schools that are excellent work places, because the teachers are supported, work collegially, and get special training about their students' needs. Some high needs schools offer signing bonuses, end-of-year bonuses, or qualify the new hire for college loan forgiveness. Accentuate the positive. After all, the Peace Corps gets lots of applicants by saying that they are "the toughest job you'll ever love." Appeal to the applicants' idealism, youthful exuberance, and sense of mission. If nothing else, recruit interviewees by letting them know that two or three successful years in your school will be a resoundingly positive experience on their resume and will enable them to find work anywhere later.

Role of Colleges and Universities

Colleges and universities offer two partnerships to school districts that need new teachers. The first partnership is with the school of education and the second with the college's career center. By accepting practicum students and student teachers, a school district creates a partnership that helps both entities. Student teachers often want to teach where they have student taught, simply because they have been welcomed and have completed a semester of part-time, supervised teaching that was successful. They feel that they know the faculty and if hired, they could "hit the ground running."

If your district is further than a manageable commute from a university, consider accepting a cohort of student teachers and supervise them with your own personnel director, assistant principal, or even a recent retiree. That way, you get some student teachers, and the university only has to send a supervisor once or twice during the semester. A cohort works well because student teachers appreciate the "safety in numbers" idea. Of course, housing is an issue to be resolved when campus and district are far apart.

If you can't bring college students to the district, share some of the district's personnel with the campus. Schools of education need speakers to talk about hiring, interviewing, the first year of teaching, teacher evaluation, and all the realities of a school year. District teachers-of-the-year make excellent speakers for campus honors nights and meetings of future teachers' associations.

Gaining momentum are also "grow your own" teacher programs that are collaborative in nature with colleges. As an alternative to relying on the traditional college graduate pool, "grow your own" programs are designed to identify potential new teachers and help them enter and complete teacher certification programs. For example, the paraprofessionals in elementary schools often decide that they want to be teachers, but need help working out schedules that allow them to be students and work part-time. Many people with earned bachelor's degrees decide to be teachers and enter post-baccalaureate licensure programs. Some states provide these candidates with provisional certification based on their degrees and the passing of tests, and then allow them to begin teaching as interns. While teaching, they pursue their coursework and must be supervised and mentored in a much more thorough manner. Again, a nearby university can provide the coursework, supervision, and the support seminars for these non-traditional students.

Starting a Future Teachers of America chapter in the high school can support students to make a decision to teach even before college. Some colleges will provide speakers for the club and may even accept a class taught in high school for college credit if the students participate in a teaching cadet program. All of these ideas can be used to put more students into the teacher education program pipeline, with the end result being a larger applicant pool. Teachers often indicate that they want to work within a 100-mile distance of where they grew up, so homegrown programs may be part of the answer. Additionally, all educators should encourage students to consider teaching. What a shame when the top students are told that they "are too smart to be teachers." The teaching profession needs the best and the brightest.

Partnerships with College Career Centers

"As districts compete among themselves for a limited supply of teachers, it makes sense to go to the source to market your district" (Gorman, 2000, p.12). While online, video, and telephone interviewing are gaining momentum in use, the opportunity to recruit in person on a college campus can still be the best way to meet a large number of new candidates in a short period of time. You can make the most of a campus teacher education job fair by doing the following:

- Ask for the approximate numbers of graduating students by field before attending the fair to see if it is worth your time to attend.
- Find out if candidate resumes or profiles are available online or in a book to preview.
- Verify that your table is reserved for you, or arrive extra early.
- If you are a personnel director, bring one or two principals along to help give 15-minute interviews.

- Bring an alumnus of the college who is now in his or her first or second year of teaching in your district. Being near the candidates in age, and being an alumnus of their program, this person has instant validity.
- Post and advertise your vacancies at the college before the fair, even if that means buying an ad in the college paper.
- Bring a bright, colorful display and have information about salary and benefits. Give out a freebie—a pen or marker with your Web site, or a disc that students can pop into their computers and "see" what it's like in your district.

In addition to the job fair, the director of a career center can help you in other ways. Don't hesitate to ask, since that person's job is dependent on how many graduates that they help to find jobs! The director of a career center can post your openings on a bulletin board, the old-fashioned kind or one that is online. They can set up individual job interview days just for your district after the fair, if your hiring needs are great. They can set up an interview day in November just for you to meet the December graduates. Of course, there are things that the director of the career center cannot do for you, such as providing you a list of the top ten students in a major, securing transcripts or releasing grades, or providing access to identifying information such as age or ethnicity (American Association for Employment in Education, 2000).

Online Recruitment

Online recruitment can take four venues—your district's Web site, use of college Web sites for postings, state Web sites, and national/international Web sites. Of course, since the Web is "out there," use of any of these sites may make your postings available to international candidates as well. Since today's college seniors have been using on-line resources since elementary school, they may not look any further than Web sites for job openings. Head lists the following five steps to designing an effective teacher recruitment Web site for a district:

- Don't wait to set up your Web site. Get basic information on-line and then build. Develop a very visible link on your district home page to a page containing information for teachers seeking a position.
- Identify all information you want a teacher to find when he or she clicks on your Web site. Contact information, information about your city and geographical area, etc.
- Set all this up as a special page just for teachers looking for positions. Include the word "Teachers" or "Educators" in big letters!
- Include access to your application online.
- Get your site connected so teachers and career services offices will find it (2000. p. 6-7).

With your district Web site advertising all the specifics, you can then turn back to the college career center for their help in posting openings. One of the easiest ways to find the Web site of the career center of a neighboring university is to use any search engine and type in "career center" and the name of the university. A quick phone call to the career center will probably answer all of your questions about how job postings are made, how long they stay up, and if any fees are associated with posting. Be sure and ask about posting in their newsletters, or having a paper flyer tacked to a real bulletin board. Yes, students at some colleges still read paper flyers, too.

If you know that the neighboring college or university cannot supply all of your needs, or if you simply want to cast a wider net for the best possible new teachers, try the online job postings for your state. The best way to find your state site is to go to www.uky.edu/Education/TEP/usjobs.html and then click on your state, or go to www.teaching-jobs.org for a clearinghouse of Web sites. It may take a little searching, but many states now have postings of all the teaching openings in the state on one site. See, for example, www.teach-georgia.org for Georgia or www.tasanet.org/educatorsjobbank for Texas. Student teachers are indeed reading these sites, as are certified teachers who move from another state. When you use the state's Web site, you can probably get a link from your posted ad there to your district Web site.

Lastly, there are national clearinghouse-type sites to match your district's needs with teachers who are seeking positions. Teachers-teachers.com is an example of a Web site designed to match districts and candidates. The www.teachers-teachers.com site is offered free of charge to candidates, but districts are charged for the service based upon their size. A similar site is www.teacherssupportnetwork.com. More sites may be appearing every year.

Professional Associations

Professional networks have their own sites for job seekers, and those can help you to find candidates. For example, the Council for Exceptional Children has "career connections" on its Web site, www.cec.sped.org. There is a jobs page on the American Council for the Teaching of Foreign Languages site, www.actfl.org. Both the National Council for Teachers of English and the National Council for

Teachers of Mathematics accept job postings for their respective Web sites, www.ncte.org and www.nctm.org. If online job postings don't offer you enough possibilities, you may go in person to a conference sponsored by a professional organization and recruit new teachers there. The honor societies in education, Kappa Delta Pi (www.kdp.org) and Phi Delta Kappa (www.pdkintl.org), also offer job recruitment opportunities.

BBI as a Recruitment Tool

"To predict how candidates might perform as employees, companies are asking about their previous performances—and getting data that lead to superior hiring decisions" (Beebe 1996, p. 40).

How is your interviewing style a recruitment tool? New teachers want to be treated professionally, and BBI uses questions about specific teaching skills and experiences. With BBI, there are not hypothetical questions or the old "tell me about yourself" questions. Candidates who are interviewed with BBI should leave the interview feeling that their teaching is what matters, not what high school they graduated from or whether or not a school board member knows a relative of theirs. Setting the tone from the very beginning of a candidate's visit to your district may be what wins that candidate over. Today's student teachers are savvy enough to know that if a district doesn't seem respectful, business-like, and professional at the interview when they are trying to impress, that the treatment of new hires after the "wooing" is over may be quite low.

The premise of BBI is that past behavior is the best predictor of future performance. If the district is professional, asking pertinent questions, and listening for "best practice" answers in interviews, then candidates are reassured that the day-to-day practices of the district will probably be professional as well.

Of course, a big part of recruitment is simply providing all who apply with correct, timely information about interviews and decisions. The best interview cannot win a candidate who was treated unprofessionally by office staff, or who had to wait longer than expected to hear back from the interviewer. While you are getting a first impression of a candidate from the paperwork and communications that happen before an interview, the candidate is also getting an impression of you as an employer. How paperwork is handled can be a part of the recruitment process itself.

Chapter 3
Evaluating the Pre-Interview Paperwork

The concept of previous behavior being the best predictor of future performance can also be applied to evaluating candidates' paperwork. Today's students are taught by their professors and their campus career centers how to write cover letters and resumes, so the paperwork going to future employers should look better than ever before. Additionally, word processing has made it even easier to produce paperwork that is free of grammatical and spelling errors. If candidates send out letters and resumes with weak content or poor presentation, that is an indicator of their lack of attention to detail, or perhaps they skipped the classes and seminars on how to prepare the paperwork!

The Cover Letter

The cover letter allows the candidate to introduce himself or herself to the potential employer. It should sell the candidate in a succinct and businesslike format. The cover letter should be an example of a candidate's best possible work—both in content and form. If you are hiring a teacher to teach paragraph writing to sixth-graders, the paragraphs in the teacher's letter should be model ones. The letter should be just one page in length. The pertinent information should be easy to find and should include:

- the date written,
- the current address of the candidate,
- how the candidate became aware of the opening,
- which job the applicant is applying for,
- indication of full certification obtained or anticipated graduation/completion date,
- at least one or two relevant facts about previous teaching experience,
- something that makes this candidate stand out in a positive manner,
- candidate's interest in your district, and
- clear information about how the candidate can be reached (Clement, 2003).

Just as the above list tells what to look for, there are things that should NOT be in the cover letter. Some call these items "red flags," as they may be indicators of deeper concerns. This list includes:

- spelling, grammar, or punctuation errors,
- an illegible signature,
- writing a cover letter that is entirely too long, and
- a letter that is not businesslike, but more of a creative art project (some teachers have sent construction paper with paragraphs and art work glued on).

As one principal said, "I want to be able to read the signature on the cover letter. If I can't, how will the students be able to read the teacher's comments on their papers?"

In my work with employers in education, I have heard debate over some of the issues listed, such as the signature issue. Each employer must decide for himself or herself on these issues, but it can be argued that a candidate with an illegible signature on a cover letter will not be able to write legibly on the board or overhead projector. Also, if this is how the candidate sends out formal correspondence, it is the predictor of how their parent letters and notes home will look. As an employer, you will be called by parents who cannot read the note their child's teacher sent home!

How important is it that the candidate indicates how they heard of the opening and write of their interest in your district? Candidates who indicate reading your ad on a Web site are also indicating some technology knowledge. Those who indicate that a supervising teacher informed them of the opening may already have ties to and experience in the area. Candidates who indicate their interest in your specific school or district may have a valid reason for wanting to be there—and they may stay when hired. Teaching can be marketed as a "family-friendly" profession because of the vacation time, work day, and benefits, so candidates who want to be in a specific geographic area may want to be there because their families are already there and they can't or don't want to relocate.

How can you evaluate the cover letter objectively? Create an instrument that lists the factors you deem most important and give them a numeric or categorical rating. Categories can be quite simple, using unacceptable, acceptable, and target. Target means that it caught your attention and stood out. A target cover letter wows the employer and puts the candidate at the top of the pile for consideration.

Table 3.1. Evaluating the Cover Letter (Categorical Rating)			
	Unacceptable	Acceptable	Target
Certification			
Relevant facts			
Interest in position			
Spelling, punctuation, grammar			
Overall presentation			

Table 3.2. Evaluating the Cover Letter (Numeric Rating)					
(Rated on a scale of 1 to 5, where 1 indicates no information or poor and 5 indicates excellence)					
Certification	1	2	3	4	5
Relevant facts	1	2	3	4	5
Interest in position	1	2	3	4	5
Spelling, punctuation, grammar	1	2	3	4	5
Overall presentation	1	2	3	4	5

Evaluating the Resume

Today's students get even more training in how to write a resume than they do in how to write a cover letter, so resumes that go out to employers should look professional. Before reading any resumes, create a list of what you need to know from the resume and decide on an evaluation instrument that will be easy to use while reading them.

A complete resume should include:
- all pertinent contact information, including information for after graduation,
- the candidate's job objective and/or certification areas,
- educational degrees,
- teaching experience,
- other work experiences,
- professional association memberships and/or college awards, and
- availability of references or credentials.

The following should not be included in or with the resume:
- a photo,
- personal information such as age, sex, race, marital status,
- family information, such as number of children, and
- physical description (people in the 1960s and 1970s included height and weight!).

Red flags can exist on resumes as well. If a candidate has gaps in schooling or previous work experience, why are those gaps there? A traditional college-aged student who takes a year off to travel abroad or do volunteer work will include that information as it is highly relevant to teaching. Long, unexplained gaps are not positive signs on a resume. Debate exists about the length of time to get through college today. Many students take the 5-year plan for a bachelor's degree because they are working 20 or more hours a week at a job. Many students often transfer one or more times before settling into a college setting that works for them. However, attending four institutions over a 6½ year period to earn a bachelor's degree may be an indicator of lack of perseverance on the part of the applicant. An applicant who has taught for only a semester or year at several schools should explain why their stays were so short at those schools, or that might be indicative of a problem.

Perhaps the most important problem that can be found on a resume would be a statement that is contradicted by other paperwork. If a resume states a grade point average of 3.7 and the transcripts indicate a 3.1 that is a concern. If the resume states certification in two areas and a check of transcripts indicates only one area with incomplete coursework in the second, the candidate is not being truthful.

The presentation of the resume should look professional, with no spelling errors or grammatical mistakes. In essence, the resume should look polished. Again, the candidate is trying to sell himself or herself, and if their best presentational work doesn't look good, how will their everyday work look? Some candidates use desktop publishing programs to create four-page resumes that look like brochures complete with graphics. As a professor, I tell students that this type of creativity is not expected, or even appreciated for the resume. If a teacher uses desktop publishing to create newsletters for classes, put that line on the resume and bring a sample in a portfolio to the interview.

To evaluate a resume, look at both content and presentation. How do you evaluate educational background? You have to decide how to rate the degree earned, or if just earning the degree is enough. There is more gray area to evaluate on a resume than a cover letter. For example, should the degree from an Ivy League school rate better than one from a small state university you have never heard of? Perhaps a good criterion is to simply ask yourself if education and teaching experience match the current job opening. Should lack of awards in college be a detractor from giving the candidate an interview? Start to plan your criteria, based on the needs of the position.

Table 3.3. Evaluating the Resume			
	Unacceptable	Acceptable	Target
Resume presentation is clear/easy to read			
Certification matches job opening			
Educational background matches job need			
Teaching experience matches job need			
Professional memberships/awards			

These same criteria can be put on a scale of 1 to 5, as well.

Letters of Recommendation

Candidates simply do not ask people to write a letter if they feel that the writer will not write an excellent one. College professors who will not say all positives in a letter generally tell students that they must find someone else to write a letter for them. So, it can almost be assumed that letters of recommendation are going to be glowing. With this in mind, the letters of recommendation can still inform the employer about the candidate.

What a target letter should reveal about the candidate:
Susan's ability to manage a class is exceptionally strong. To evidence this, she invited me to see her teach on the Friday afternoon before spring break. When I suggested that she might not want her college supervisor there at the time, she insisted that she *did* want me there—to specifically see how she handled wrapping up a 9-weeks and leading a game on the afternoon before break. It went beautifully. If she can handle a class at this crucial time, she can handle anything.

An acceptable letter might look like this:
John has completed a unique year-long student teaching experience, spending two semesters with one sixth-grade teacher. He completed all assignments and taught a unit on geometry. His skills in front of the class improved greatly from my first visit to my last. He is ready to start teaching in his first classroom.

Unacceptable letters have red flags:
I served as Beth's college supervisor during the spring semester. I worked with her on a weekly basis to help her apply what she had learned on campus to the real-world classroom. She completed the student teaching semester and remains intent upon teaching, but if hired she would need supervision and mentoring. I recommend that you interview her and talk with her two cooperating teachers at Lincoln Elementary for their evaluations as well.

What can letters tell us? First of all, if letters are missing, or if they are late because the candidate didn't give them to writers in a timely manner, that may speak to the candidate's ability to meet deadlines (or the writer's ability to do the same). If a letter does not exist from a college supervisor or a cooperating teacher and the student just completed student teaching that can indicate that neither were willing to write a letter. A letter that says that the candidate student taught and does not indicate any vignettes or special stories from that experience may be a cause for concern. Some writers will not write negatives, but will only state basic facts, such as the weeks of student teaching and the number of students taught. A letter that indicates that you should contact the cooperating teacher or college supervisor for more details may be indicative of a concern.

I personally write dozens of letters of recommendation every year. For really strong candidates, I indicate that it is a pleasure to write the letter and I include very specific examples of the candidate's teaching that I observed. I back up my glowing statements for all attributes with examples. I end by saying that the candidate is ready to teach and should be hired. For average candidates, I still write specific examples, but I end by saying that the candidate has come through a strong teacher education program and I recommend that he or she be interviewed for consideration. If a weak student teacher asks me to write a letter, I still do so, but I tell them up front that I will indicate areas in which they need to work and will recommend to the employer, that if hired, this person will need mentoring and a supportive work environment.

How will you evaluate the letters of recommendation? Your form might resemble Table 3.4.

Table 3.4. Evaluating Letters of Recommendation			
	Unacceptable	Acceptable	Target
Letters recommended candidate			
Examples of successful teaching included			
A special strength, energy, or enthusiasm mentioned			
No areas of concern			

Transcripts

For legal reasons, the employer needs the transcripts as proof of educational accomplishments. How much do grades and transcripts reveal, especially in these days of grade inflation? I once heard a principal say that employers with high grades looked for candidates with high grades, and those employers with average or low grades didn't weight grades as heavily in their hiring decisions. Do high grades make a good teacher? Are straight "A" students the most effective teachers? While no one is going to hire a new teacher solely on the basis of a grade point average, transcripts may be indicators to help you look at a student's past behavior.

It can be argued by college professors that grades are an indicator of class attendance, since attending class regularly does help raise one's grades. Virtually all professors lower grades when assignments are turned in late, so grades might also be an indicator of ability to meet deadlines. These two statements are definitely true in my own teacher education classes.

Some colleges record the courses completed and grades assigned for a semester, without listing all courses attempted and then dropped. If the transcript lists all courses attempted and those dropped, that can be an indicator of a student's inability to complete work attempted the first time. Some student transcripts show a pattern of dropping one or two courses each semester. Look for patterns in transcripts, reading the fine print about what is listed and what is omitted.

Because of grade inflation, some colleges of education no longer accept grades of D, and students must retake courses where they fail or earn a D. Therefore, grades of C are no longer average and most students earn A's and B's. A lot of C's on a transcript may be an overall indicator of weak work habits. Student teaching grades tend to be quite high for all students, as the rules for qualifying to student teach are strict and cooperating teachers are often hesitant to give low grades to student teachers. A low grade in student teaching may be indicative of a concern. The processes of grading and of evaluating someone's grades may well remain one of the most debated topics in education.

Heard at a workshop on how to hire new teachers:

Principal #1: If you want to hire a good teacher, hire a student with good grades.

Principal #2: But don't hire one with straight A's, since they never understand why some students don't learn.

Your District's Application

As you create a new district application, or use an existing one, it is good to remember that, if the application is to be used for

Table 3.5. Evaluating the Candidate Paperwork			
	Unacceptable	Acceptable	Target
The Cover Letter			
Certification			
Relevant facts			
Interest in position			
Spelling, punctuation, grammar			
Overall presentation			
The Resume			
Resume presentation is clear/easy to read			
Certification matches job opening			
Educational background matches job need			
Teaching experience matches job need			
Professional memberships/awards			

evaluative purposes, there should be a way to evaluate whatever you ask candidates to write on the application. Your district application may be one that is just for administrative use, needing the applicant's address, emergency contact numbers, addresses of references, and a list of former employers.

Table 3.5. Evaluating the Candidate Paperwork *(continued)*			
	Unacceptable	Acceptable	Target
Letters of Recommendation			
Letters recommended candidate			
Examples of successful teaching included			
A special strength, energy, or enthusiasm mentioned			
No areas of concern			
Transcripts			
Grades			
No areas/patterns of concern			
District Application *(if used for evaluation)*			
Lesson plan			
Statement of philosophy			
Total number of each category, looking for high numbers of "target".			

If the district application calls for a statement of philosophy and/or sample lesson plans, decide in advance how these will be evaluated, and how much these count toward inviting the candidate for an on-site interview.

Summary of Paperwork Issues

A candidate's cover letter, resume, and letters of recommendation are meant to present the candidate's skills, experiences, and interests in the most positive way possible. As an employer, the paperwork gives you the first impression of the candidate and helps you to begin the sorting process. There may be candidates who appear wonderfully skilled on paper, but who cannot stand up in front of a class and teach. Some candidates may have weaker paperwork, but are skillful in their work with students.

The truth is that today's teachers must be able to document their work, and candidates who can provide strong documentation of their college careers can probably prepare equally good documentation needed in their teaching careers. Hence, it is a behavior-based assessment. While the paperwork is the introduction, and wins the candidate the interview, it is the interview that will provide the most insight about whether the candidate can do the job.

Sorting the Paperwork (Practice Activity)

You need to hire a new middle school (6th, 7th, and 8th) science teacher. You have to choose only one from the following three resumes to interview, since you already have two other finalists. Which would you choose to interview and why?

Candidate A
- Fully certified for middle grades language arts and science.
- Recent graduate, just finished a semester of student teaching in a self-contained sixth-grade classroom where she taught all classes.

- GPA: 2.97/4.0; B. S. in Middle Grades Education
- No awards or extracurricular activities; indicated she worked 12 hours a week in dorm's food service throughout college.
- Summer job: Three summers as Girl Scout camp counselor, same camp each summer.

Candidate B
- Fully certified for middle grades math and science.
- Out of college for 8 years. Taught 1 year, urban district. Out 2 years. Taught 1 semester (suburban district). Out 1 year. Taught 1 year (private school). Out 1½ years. Taught 1 year (nearby district).
- GPA 3.4/4.0; B. S. in Middle Grades Education
- Undergraduate: Two scholarships, traveled to Europe with college choir.
- Lists that she has two children and has been a volunteer at church day care and Vacation Bible School.
- Has taken two courses since college in special education and one in Spanish.

Candidate C
- Provisionally certified (passed state testing), seeking an internship where she can begin teaching full-time and complete coursework over the next school year and summer.
- Out of college for 7 years, worked 5 of those years as a quality control technician at food processing plant/2 years as a county extension agent in home economics and still employed there.
- GPA: 3.9/4.0; Bachelor's degree in Biology with a minor in Chemistry

- Undergraduate: Three science awards, membership in two honor societies and Governor's scholar for 3 years.
- Extracurricular activities: Tennis (varsity); aerobics instructor; swim instructor.
- Has taken four education courses through community college and regional office of education.

Are there red flags for any of the candidates that make you want to eliminate them?

- Does candidate A's grade point average seem too low?
- Should candidate B's short stays in each job be a concern? Is this a behavior pattern that might predict future performance?
- Candidate C seems very bright and well-rounded, but is only provisionally certified.

What are the special skills that make you want to consider each candidate?

- Candidate A has three summers of experience working with Girl Scouts.
- Candidate B has added hours to her degree work in special education and Spanish; she has experience in diverse settings (urban, suburban, and local).
- Candidate C can probably coach tennis and swimming, and can teach aerobics to the faculty in a staff development setting.

Choose the candidate who will get the interview and explain your choice.

Chapter 4
Creation of the Behavior-Based Interviewing Questions

Ask 10 teachers what qualities make a good teacher and you will probably get 10 different answers. Ask 10 principals and you will receive another 10 answers. Professors of education, educational theorists, and even politicians will have their own list of characteristics of effective teachers. Fortunately, there is some overlap!

More literature exists about the knowledge base of teaching than ever before. Textbooks used in introductory classes for teacher education include lists of characteristics of good teachers. One introductory book lists the following:

- commitment to students and their learning,
- knowledge of subjects and how to convey content to students,
- ability to manage and monitor student learning,
- ability to think about teaching and learn from experiences, and
- participation in learning communities (Wiseman, et al., 2002).

In their introductory education text, Parkay and Stanford (2004) write that "...teachers are expected to be proficient in the use of instructional strategies, curriculum materials, advanced educational technologies, and classroom management techniques" (p. 27).

Additionally, effective teachers "…have a thorough understanding of the developmental levels of their students and of the content they teach" (p. 27). Teachers do all of this while accepting students from diverse backgrounds and believing in the potential of all students.

Noted educator Harry Wong writes that an effective teacher:
- has positive expectations for student success,
- is an extremely good classroom manager, and
- knows how to design lessons for student mastery (Wong & Wong, 2004, p. 9).

Teaching is such a complex task that the list of traits for effective teachers can become quite lengthy. McEwan (2002) writes of the 10 traits of highly effective teachers by dividing the traits into three categories: personal traits that indicate character; teaching traits that get results; and intellectual traits that demonstrate knowledge, curiosity, and awareness (191-193). Stronge and Hindman (2003) list 27 qualities of teacher effectiveness as they relate to selecting candidates, and organize their qualities into six domains. The domains are: prerequisites of effective teachers, the teacher as a person, classroom management and organization, organizing of instruction, implementing instruction, and monitoring student progress and potential (2003, p. 50).

Creation of Questions Based on Teacher Effectiveness

A key component in using BBI is to write the best possible questions. For teacher selection, these questions must be based on the factors that indicate teacher effectiveness, and then they must be worded in a way that will allow for evaluation of the answers. Answers will be evaluated to see if the candidate has had past experience with the factor, and if so, if that experience was one where the candidate understood what happened and can replicate the effective teaching practice when hired.

"Skillful questioning during the interview, however, can reveal behavior patterns that indicate with high predictability whether the candidate can, or would, perform the job as required" (Beebe, 1996, p. 42).

To begin the process of the creation of questions, start with the basic factors of teacher effectiveness, using research that has already been done in the field, and your own experience. Questions for teachers of all grade-levels and subjects will include ones on the following topics:

- curriculum,
- planning,
- methods,
- classroom management,
- assessment and grading,
- meeting the needs of individual students,
- communication with parents and others, and
- professionalism.

With the factors decided, write the questions in a manner to elicit a response where the candidate describes past work and experiences.

Creation of Questions for Specific Grade-Levels or Subjects

In order to be effective in a certain teaching position, a candidate needs specific skills and experiences. In hiring preschool teachers, issues of child development may be most important. For elementary education positions, the techniques used for teaching reading may constitute a

Table 4.1. Generic Interview Questions for All Teachers

Curriculum

- How have the national and state standards for teaching this subject area guided your teaching?
- What are important curricular topics for this grade and subject area?
- Describe a 2-week unit you have taught.

Planning

- Describe how you plan a lesson.
- Tell me about a time when you wrote a lesson plan that went well and a time when a plan did not go well. What was the difference?
- What are some of your favorite ways to begin and end a class?

Methods

- Describe how you teach a lesson.
- What specific teaching methods have you used in the past and why are they in your repertoire?
- Which methods have you found to work best with students in the past, and why?
- Describe how you have integrated technology into your lessons.

Classroom Management

- Describe a classroom that you liked where you have observed or taught. What components of that room would you bring to your new classroom?
- What kinds of rules, positives, and consequences are appropriate for students at this age?
- What should be done the first week of school for starting a new school year?

Table 4.1. Generic Interview Questions for All Teachers *(continued)*

Assessment and Grading

- Describe a typical homework assignment that you have used in the past.
- What have you done to increase the students' completion rate of homework?
- Describe a grading system that you would implement in this new position.
- While a lesson is ongoing, how can you tell if students are "getting" the new material?

Meeting the Needs of Individual Students

- Describe an approach that you have used to help slow learners succeed.
- What modifications have you made to lessons to assist special education or language minority students?
- How can you help to promote tolerance and acceptance among your students?

Communication with Parents and Others

- Describe positive parent communications that you have used in the past.
- Tell me about a time when you discussed an issue with a parent and then the students' behavior or academic progress changed.

Professionalism

- How do you evaluate your teaching?
- Describe a time when you knew that you had achieved success with students.
- How do you stay current with the trends and issues in education and in your subject-matter field(s)?

large part of the interview. Determine what skills and experiences are crucial for the position, and then create the questions that will elicit appropriate responses. Sample questions for preschool and elementary school positions are listed on Table 4.2 and Table 4.3.

Many principals have commented, "But high school teaching is different than middle school and elementary teaching is different than every other level. When will the personnel director in the central office learn that?"

What's Important in Hiring Middle School Teachers?

If elementary teachers choose their profession because they love children, and secondary teachers because their love their subject matter, what makes middle school teachers choose this age level? And what special skills must the middle grades teacher possess? Do they have to be a little "wild and crazy" and a little like "Mother Goose," to be effective (Willems & Clifford, 1999)? Team-teaching, collaboration, and curriculum integration may be crucial elements of the knowledge base for middle grades teachers. Additionally, they need to be well-versed in the needs of adolescents and the developmental stages of this age group. Hence, interview questions for middle school teachers can be written with these special considerations in mind (see Table 4.4).

But High School Teaching is Different

Today's high school students may be socially mature beyond their years, but they may also be academically behind compared to previous generations. National tests scores, college entrance, and preparation for the world of work are all part of the high school experience. Of course, football games, homecoming, and pep rallies make some high schools look like ones of the 1950s during the fall semester. What's different about the skills needed to teach high school? Subject matter expertise remains critical in hiring high school teachers, but so does the ability to motivate and manage students who may be raising children of their own and working long hours while still in school. High school teachers are increasingly accountable for raising the graduation rate while maintaining high standards. As one high school teacher said, "This job is NOT for the faint of heart." Interview questions will need to focus on subject matter, methods of teaching, motivating, and managing, as well as assessment (see Table 4.5).

Additionally, a set of questions may be needed for each area of the high school curriculum. If interviewing a candidate for a foreign language position, part of the interview may need to be completed by another language teacher to verify the candidate's fluency. These candidates need to be asked about their experience teaching the language in a total immersion setting, as opposed to teaching the foreign language while using English. High school employers may want to include departmental chairs or committees in writing these questions and in the interview process.

BBI Questions for Special Education

Because many features of special education programs are guided by federal and state mandates, this field has been characterized with its own vocabulary and uniqueness. Special education teachers need specific skills and knowledge, so questions must be crafted to elicit the candidate's knowledge and experience in the area in which they will be teaching. A list of generic special education questions will help you to start crafting your questions (see Table 4.6).

Table 4.2. Sample Questions for Preschool

Child Development

- Explain a task that might be developmentally inappropriate for a 3-year old, yet could be done easily by a kindergarten student.
- What have you done in the past to help a child who is frustrated that he or she cannot complete a task that others in the class can accomplish?

Curriculum

- What are important curricular topics for the preschool student?
- What have you used from the national and state standards to guide your teaching?

Planning

- Describe a successful lesson you have taught.
- Tell me about a time when you ran out of time to finish a lesson. What did you do and how did the children react?
- What are tried-and-true ways to get the attention of young children?

Classroom Organization and Management

- What special safety precautions must be considered when working with the youngest students (2- or 3-year olds)?
- What kinds of rules and consequences have you implemented in a classroom of 4-year olds?
- What do young children consider to be rewards?
- Tell me about a time when a child tested the limits you set. What did you do and what were the results?

Table 4.2. Sample Questions for Preschool *(continued)*

Assessment and Individual Needs

- How have you assessed students' progress?
- Young children need a lot of attention. How have you created opportunities to individualize the attention you give to children in your room?
- What modifications have you made to accommodate learning disabilities or language minority children in your room?

Communication with Parents/Professionalism

- Describe a successful parent conference you have conducted.
- What have you read or studied recently that led to a change in your classroom teaching or work with children?

Designing Questions for the Non-Fully Certified Teacher Applicant

"This spring on many college campuses, something absolutely remarkable happened: Talented young people lined up by the scores to teach lower-income kids in urban and rural public schools. In years past, investment banks like Goldman Sachs were the recruiting powerhouses at top campuses; this year, they were joined by Teach for America, a program that expresses the fresh idealism and social values of this new generation" (Gergen, 2005, p. 78).

Teacher shortages in parts of the country and in certain teaching fields have led some districts to hire non-fully certified teachers. Each state creates its own rules regarding the training a candidate must have before entering a classroom, which varies from all coursework except student teaching to no coursework and only the successful

Table 4.3. Sample Questions for Elementary Education (K-6)

Reading/Literacy

- Describe how you have taught reading in the past.
- Describe your experiences teaching phonics.
- Describe your experiences teaching with whole language.
- Describe your experiences teaching with a balanced literacy approach.
- Name and describe any specific reading package that you have taught with in the past (for example, directed reading instruction or a specific textbook publisher).

Methods/Subject Integration

- Describe successful techniques that you have used to help students learn and improve their writing.
- Describe how you have used manipulatives to teach a lesson.
- Describe any concept that you have taught and how you taught that concept.
- How have you integrated science and reading? Social studies and reading?
- How have you used small group work successfully with this age group?

Assessment

- How have you prepared students for standardized tests?
- What is your experience using assessments other than tests with students?
- How have you used portfolios to assess student progress?

Table 4.3. Sample Questions for Elementary Education (K-6) (continued)

- Describe your experiences with anecdotal records or running records to assess reading achievement.
- How can you tell that students are actively engaged in learning without testing or assigning a grade to an activity?

Classroom Organization/Management

- Describe how your classroom can be a print-rich environment for students.
- What specific room arrangements have you created and why have they worked?
- How do you transition students from one activity/subject to the next successfully?
- Describe your movement in the classroom for a typical morning.
- How have you integrated movement and music into your classroom routines?
- What rewards and consequences have worked well with this age group?

Communication and Working with Peers

- Describe a time when you were co-teaching with another teacher or paraprofessional in the classroom.
- Describe your experiences planning with other teachers.
- Describe the types of communications that are effective to share with parents.
- What challenges have you encountered in communicating with parents and how have you dealt with those challenges?

Table 4.4. Sample Questions for Middle School

Collaboration

- Tell me about a time when you have worked on a teaching team.
- What are some advantages of team planning for working with and motivating students?
- Describe your experiences of working in a "school within a school" concept.

Curriculum

- Share an example you have seen or used for integrating writing across the curriculum.
- How have you integrated math into other subject areas?
- The improvement of students' reading skills is important during middle school. Tell about your experiences teaching reading directly, or how you have integrated reading strategies into other subject areas.

Teaching Methods

- Games can be intrinsically motivating to middle grades students. How have you used games to motivate students in your classes? Have you encountered problems with the use of games, and how did you resolve the problem?
- Describe any opportunity you have had to give students an outside audience for their work (presentations, writings, Web site).
- Describe a lesson that you have taught that helped prepare your students for high school.
- How do your teaching strategies help prepare students for taking standardized tests?

Student Needs

- What is a typical concern/worry that middle school students bring to their teachers as advisors/counselors and how have you dealt with such a concern?
- How have you found backup help for a student problem if you felt the issue was beyond your area of expertise?

Table 4.4. Sample Questions for Middle School *(continued)*

- Adolescents need time for talking and expressing their opinions. How have you built time into your day to allow students to discuss opinions, talk about topics of interest, and to "vent" their frustrations?
- Besides group discussions, how have you been able to give students opportunities to express their interests, goals, and concerns?
- Describe an activity that you have used that helps your students to de-stress.

School Climate

- What have you implemented to make your classroom welcoming and student-friendly?
- What strategies have you used or observed to improve school climate and increase student attendance?
- Do you have a special skill or interest that you have shared with students in an exploratory class or homeroom?

Classroom Management

- Much has been written about logical consequences for student misbehaviors. Describe a common misbehavior seen in middle school and what a logical consequence for the behavior might be.
- How have you involved students in discussion of rules, consequences, and rewards? Why is this step of establishing a management plan so important to middle school students?
- What words or phrases have become typical positive reinforcements in your teaching vocabulary and how do middle school students respond to this type of reinforcement?

Communication and Professionalism

- How much information do you share about yourself with students during the first days of school? Why?
- Tell about a challenging parent conference that you were involved in and how that conference was resolved.

Table 4.5. Sample Questions for High School

Curriculum

- How have you interested students in your subject field?
- Give an example of how you can relate your subject to something of relevance to today's teenagers.
- How have you supplemented the textbook in your classes?
- Give an example of a state or national standard and how you teach to that standard in your class.
- What is a current trend in the teaching of this subject and how have you dealt with this trend?

Motivation

- Describe how you become acquainted with your students at the beginning of a new semester.
- How have you encouraged students to stay in high school and graduate?
- What kinds of stressors do today's high school students face and how have you helped them cope with their concerns?
- How have you encouraged and met the needs of gifted, talented, and advanced students in your classes?

Methods

- Describe the student teaching or teaching experiences you have had with traditional 50-minute classes and with blocked scheduling.
- Describe a unit or syllabus that you have written for a 2-week period of time for a class. What was included?
- Describe the methods that you use most frequently to teach a lesson.
- Describe any group work or projects that you use with students.

Table 4.5. Sample Questions for High School *(continued)*

- How have you successfully prepared students for standardized tests, graduation tests, or end-of-course tests?

Communication with Colleagues, Parents, and Students

- How have you kept your principal, curriculum director, and/or department head informed of special lessons and activities in your classes?
- How have you communicated long-range plans to students and parents?
- How have you supported students or become better acquainted with students through extracurricular activities?

Assessment and Management

- On the first day of class, how do you introduce yourself to the students? How much of your personal life do you share with high school students?
- Explain your grading scale as though you were explaining it to students the first week of class.
- Explain your classroom management plan as though you were explaining it to students the first week of class.
- Describe a time when a student challenged your authority and how you reacted.
- Describe a time when a student challenged your knowledge of the subject and how you reacted.

Other

- How have you integrated technology into your high school classes? What has worked well with students?
- Describe a personal problem that a student has brought to you and how you dealt with that situation.

Table 4.6. Sample Questions for Special Education (All Grade Levels)

Populations

• Describe your past experiences with exceptional learners. Be specific.

• Describe your experiences with students exhibiting ADD and ADHD. What strategies were most effective for those students?

• Describe your work with students exhibiting marked impulsivity.

• Describe your work with students with _____ (insert a specific disability here).

Settings

• Describe your experiences with mainstreaming as a special education teacher working with a classroom teacher.

• Describe your experiences with full inclusion as a special education teacher working with a classroom teacher.

• Describe your experiences as a teacher in a pull-out program.

• Describe how you have worked with other professionals to help a student through collaborative consultation.

---

completion of tests. See your state Web site for listings of individual state requirements.

Districts seeking to hire non-fully certified teaching personnel are looking for true subject matter experts—chemists who want to teach chemistry, engineers who want to teach math, and native speakers of world languages who can teach others to speak the language. However, some of these candidates will have had no background in methods, management, or educational psychology. They may be in for a surprise when they face the real, live students of today's classrooms.

Table 4.6. Sample Questions for Special Education (All Grade Levels) *(continued)*

- Describe your work with one student's Individualized Education Program (IEP).

Methods

- Describe how you have incorporated technology into lessons for exceptional children.
- How have you modified lessons for exceptional learners?
- How have you modified tests for exceptional learners?
- How have you modified a physical environment feature to assist a child?

Communication

- Describe a parent conference that you have observed or participated in regarding an exceptional child. What went well? What would you change?
- Describe a positive meeting between a special education teacher and a classroom teacher about a specific child. What went well? What would you change?

Candidates who are not fully certified may be asked the regular set of questions for their grade level. However, if they are entering teaching through a test-out option—a program where they did not student teach, or a program where they begin teaching and then take coursework—they simply will not know the answers to BBI-type questions. If provisionally certified people are needed to fill teaching positions, the employer needs to attempt to assess the candidate's overall education and work background, including questions about any past experiences with children and the candidate's attitude toward the teaching profession (see Table 4.7).

Table 4.7. Sample Questions for Non-Fully Certified Teachers (Any Subject or Grade Level)

Entrance into Teaching

- Why are you choosing to enter teaching through a provisional route, without being fully certified?
- What personal characteristics and background do you possess that will help you to succeed in teaching?

Education—Past and Present

- Tell me about your bachelor's degree and the specifics of your knowledge of the subject(s) you will teach.
- Describe your route to provisional certification—testing, coursework, and field experiences. Now describe your proposed route to full certification.
- What experiences in classrooms have you had with students this age?
- What experiences have you had with students of this age outside of classrooms?
- What are you currently reading and studying to learn about the trends and issues in education and in your subject matter field(s)?

Past Work Experience

- In your previous jobs, what types of organizational skills did you use?
- Tell about a time when you planned and implemented an activity, meeting, or event.
- What kinds of assessment did you conduct in your previous work?
- How did you know that you were successful in your past job?

Table 4.7. Sample Questions for Non-Fully Certified Teachers (Any Subject or Grade Level) *(continued)*

- Tell about communications you implemented with your past boss and peers.
- Tell about experiences that you have had establishing and enforcing rules in a work setting.
- Describe your role in being a leader or innovator in your previous jobs.

About the Teaching Profession

- What does the general public believe about education, teachers, and schools? What do you believe about education, teachers, and schools?
- If you were to encounter negativity on the part of other teachers in your building because you are not fully certified, how might you combat that negativity?
- What is your response to this statement: Teaching is an easy job for those who want to work from 8 to 4, Monday through Friday.

Use of Existing Standards to Create Interview Questions

While debate continues about the necessary skills and dispositions to be an effective teacher, there are established standards for the preparation of teachers. One set of standards is that of the Interstate New Teacher Assessment and Support Consortium (INTASC). The IN-TASC Standards for Beginning Teacher Licensing and Development (Parkay & Stanford, 2004) consist of 10 standards ranging from knowledge of subject matter to partnerships with colleagues, parents, and community. The 10 standards are listed here with BBI questions that address the skills of each standard.

Questions Based on the INTASC Standards

1. Knowledge of subject matter: The teacher understands the central concepts, tools of inquiry, and structures of the subject being taught and can create learning experiences that make these aspects of subject matter meaningful for students.
    *   Describe an activity, lesson, or project that your students have done that was successful and explain why it was successful.
    *   Describe a topic considered hard to teach in your field and a lesson that you have used that students enjoyed on this topic.

2. Knowledge of human development and learning: The teacher understands how children learn and develop, and can provide learning opportunities that support their intellectual, social and personal development.
    *   Describe an activity or lesson that was successful with an age group that you have taught, and then explain why this same lesson would not work with older or younger students.
    *   Describe a lesson where you have integrated a social skill into an academic lesson.

3. Adapting instruction for individual needs: The teacher understands how students differ in their approaches to learning and creates instructional opportunities that are adapted to diverse learners.
    *   Describe a lesson that you have taught that combined auditory, visual, and/or kinesthetic teaching strategies.

- Describe modifications that you have made to an assignment or test so that a student could master the material successfully in spite of an exceptionality.

4. Multiple instructional strategies: The teacher uses various instructional strategies to encourage students' development of critical thinking, problem solving, and performance skills.
   - Describe a lesson where you used higher order questions to challenge students.
   - Describe an activity that you have implemented where students "do" something with material from a textbook other than just answer questions.

5. Classroom motivation and management: The teacher uses an understanding of individual and group motivation and behavior to create a learning environment that encourages positive social interaction, active engagement in learning, and self-motivation.
   - How do you set up a classroom routine to facilitate "time on task"?
   - Describe how your classroom management plan has worked to improve the behavior of an individual student.

6. Communication skills: The teacher uses knowledge of effective verbal, nonverbal, and media communication techniques to foster active inquiry, collaboration, and supportive interaction in the classroom.
   - Explain how you have used technology or other visuals to enhance a lesson.
   - How can you tell that students hear and understand your directions, lesson input, and questions?

7. Instructional planning skills: The teacher plans instruction based upon knowledge of subject matter, the students, the community, and curriculum goals.

    • Describe a state or national standard in your subject field and how you planned a lesson to meet that standard.

    • Tell about your long-term planning. How do you plan a unit keeping national, state, and district goals in mind?

8. Assessment of student learning: The teacher understands and uses formal and informal assessment strategies to evaluate and ensure the continuous intellectual, social, and physical development of the learner.

    • Describe a grading scale that works well for one subject in your grade area.

    • Besides written tests, how have you assessed student work?

9. Professional commitment and responsibility: The teacher is a reflective practitioner who continually evaluates the effects of his or her choices and actions on others (students, parents, and other professionals in the learning community) and who actively seeks out opportunities to grow professionally.

    • In college or during your previous teaching experiences, what course or professional development opportunity has been most beneficial to you? Why?

    • In what organizations do you maintain membership and what materials do you read to stay current in your field?

10. Partnerships: The teacher fosters relationships with school colleagues, parents, and agencies in the larger community to support students' learning and well-being.

- Describe positive parent involvement or community involvement programs that you have worked with or observed.
- Describe a successful way to communicate with colleagues or with a principal.

Writing More Questions Based on Other Research

In his book, *Teachers Wanted: Attracting and Retaining New Teachers*, Daniel Heller (2004) writes, "The way to change a school is through the hiring process" (p. 10) and "A teacher new to your school should find no surprises" (p. 48). He says that employers need to be brutally honest with potential new hires about the student population, the school needs, and problems. He then outlines what to look for in a first interview with a candidate. His list includes the following:

- Attitude: likes kids, positive, flexible, supportive, understands need to work with parents;
- Pedagogy: student-centered, multiple techniques, can match technique to student, good knowledge base in field;
- Learner: reflective thinker, comfortable with risks, can fail and try again, accepts criticism, desire to learn and improve;
- Management: treats students with respect, can keep students engaged, puts students at the center, can handle difficult students, handles most of own problems; and
- Collaborator: can work with others, can flow with a situation, willing to share, respectful of others.

Now, using what you have learned about BBI questions, write the questions you would use based on these five areas. Two or three questions per area should provide you with enough information to make a determination if this candidate merits a longer, more in-depth interview. As you write each question, remember to think about how a candidate could answer with past experiences and how you would evaluate the answer.

Summary

Many criteria exist for describing an effective teacher. Some have been written by national organizations, such as INTASC, while others have been developed by researchers and practitioners. Before ever inviting a candidate for an interview, the employer should envision exactly what is needed in the new hire, and develop a set of questions that ascertain the skills and past experiences of the candidate. Once the list of questions is prepared, the interviewer should consider what answers are sought and how those answers can be evaluated.

"If you don't know what your target is, you can't aim at it, and you certainly can't hit it." Mike Soltys of Allentown College of St. Francis de Sales goes on to explain why he believes the job analysis that defines the target is so essential to the entire BBI process: *"The interviewer must first know what the job entails – what functions need to be performed. Only then can he or she phrase the questions that will bring out the responses needed to determine whether the candidate has the proper qualifications to be successful working for the company. It all hangs on the job requirements,"* he says (Beebe, 1996, p. 42).

Chapter 5

Assessment and Rubrics for the Interview Questions

"You've taught us what to ask, but how do we evaluate the answers?"

The key to assessing candidate answers is simply to have questions that can be evaluated. There are no right and wrong answers to a question such as "tell me about yourself." However, when a candidate is asked to describe how he or she plans a lesson, there are responses that indicate past performance knowledge and those responses can be evaluated. For this particular question, the interviewer is looking for an answer that includes something about an introduction or focus, evidence of teacher presentation and activities for students, as well as a conclusion that assesses student learning.

If a candidate answers that he or she has studied Madeline Hunter's style of planning, as well as Barak Rosenshine's style, and has seen what other ninth-grade teachers in the schools are doing with a certain district-mandated plan, that is a start to a good answer. The candidate may then continue and say, "During student teaching I wrote plans that had to be approved by both my cooperating teacher and my college supervisor. My plans included objectives, lesson activities, and assessments. I learned to write outlines, including the questions I needed to ask about the readings, and to always make a list of the materials needed to teach the lesson. I like having plans because it lowers my stress, keeps me on track, and it's a way to make sure I'm covering what I'm supposed to cover." A really strong answer might end with, "I can't imagine not writing a plan. Who would want to waste precious teaching time?" We know that this is a strong answer, but we still need parameters for evaluating the answer.

Using PAR to Evaluate Answers

PAR is an acronym that stands for problem, action, result. Many questions that are posed to candidates really are ones about problems. Asking a candidate to "describe an approach that you have used to help slow learners succeed" implies that slow learners exist and are a concern to teachers. The candidate who has experienced students working at different rates, and has tried some interventions to help those students, will be able to discuss the problem, possible actions, and the result. Within the "result" part of the answer should be some evidence of reflection on the part of the candidate. The best reflections are ones where the candidate says, "what I learned…" or "what I will do differently next time is…."

Answers with PAR Guideline

Example #1:

> Interview question: Tell about a time when you felt your lesson didn't go as planned. What did you do and what did the students do?

> Candidate answer: I was supposed to teach a lesson to eighth-graders about solving problems in pre-algebra. I prepared carefully

with examples from the book for my lesson. I presented the new material well, but when it came time for students to practice, they asked me for some answers that I didn't know. They started to look toward the teacher and some started to talk. One boy said, "If she doesn't know, how should I?" (problem). I am not in their class every day, and I hadn't looked back at the problems from the previous day's lesson or from the next day's lesson. It seems that the math book is very linear, and each day's practice problems include previous questions and a preview of the next day. That day, I quickly used the teacher guide and just thought on my feet, too (action). I learned that I have to take into consideration the past and future lessons every time I plan. After I started doing this, the lessons went much more smoothly (result).

This is a very strong answer. If the interviewer is using a scale of unacceptable, acceptable, and target to evaluate the answers, this would be a target answer.

Example #2:

Interview question: Describe a common student misbehavior and what a logical consequence for the behavior might be.

Candidate answer: The biggest problem we have is students who blurt out answers all the time. Sixth-graders just don't know how to raise their hands anymore (problem). My cooperating teacher suggested that I do some "think, pair, share" questions to try to avoid the blurting problem (action). I was actually surprised how well this worked, and I could ask deeper questions, too. For example, I now tell my students that they will have 15 seconds to think about the answer, then 30 seconds to discuss the answer with a person seated beside them, and that after that we will need one or two groups to share their good answers. This has worked (result). In addition, I can do some simple elementary school routines for getting answers, too, like drawing a name out of a box to see who answers. I have to use variety.

Again, this is a target answer. The candidate has experience with the problem, learned about an action, took it and learned from it.

Using STAR to Evaluate Answers

A second acronym that helps you to follow candidate's answers is STAR. STAR represents situation, task, action, and result. Teacher candidates should be able to describe teaching situations, sorting out what is significant and what is not significant to the situation. With a brief description of a situation, the candidate should be able to talk about the task that had to be done, the action of implementing the task, and the results.

Answers with STAR Guideline

Example #1:

Interview question: How have you interested students in the subject field?

Candidate answer: Well, it can be tough to get juniors interested in the mandatory US history class, simply because it is required and they think that they have studied history throughout their school careers (situation). I have to make the readings and the class discussions relevant to their lives (task). One thing that I have tried is to have current events that are similar to past historical events. For example, with regard to the 2004 presidential election, I asked about other father/son historical figures and about the role of the Electoral College in how we elect a president (action). We had some lively discussions about what if they had to follow in their mother's or father's jobs, as well as about the Electoral College. I've learned that I have to bring history into the students' frame of reference to get their interest (result).

Example #2:

Interview question: Describe how you become acquainted with your students at the beginning of the school year.

Candidate answer: I student taught in a class with 24 very diverse third-graders, and I started student teaching in January, after they knew each other well and the teacher knew them well (situation). I knew that I shouldn't just rely on the teacher's comments on the students for my opinion, just as I should not listen to every complaint that other teachers in the future will have about my students. I have to get to know them for myself (task). I created an interest inventory that included favorite book, favorite toy or game, what they did in their free time, if they had a pet, and what they liked to learn in class (action). Their answers surprised me a lot. I learned that they watched some of the shows that my friends and I watch—and they were only third-graders! I learned that if they were listening to adult music and watching adult-themed TV shows, I had better not talk down to them, too (result).

PAR and STAR help to guide the interviewer to follow the candidate's answers, and hopefully those answers are going somewhere! If a candidate gets lost in answering, an interviewer may want to guide an answer with PAR or STAR. For example, if a candidate describes the teaching situation and problem at length, the interviewer may ask the candidate to now tell what action could resolve the problem and what could be learned as a result. A candidate who responds that he or she has seen the problem but honestly doesn't know how to resolve it may not be able to overcome the problem when it reappears. This is an example of someone who hasn't had the appropriate past learning experience and the future performance of this candidate will be indicative of that lack of past experience.

PAR stands for Problem, Action, Result

STAR stands for Situation, Task, Action, and Result

Ask a question and listen for the candidate to answer with succinct descriptions of problems, actions taken, and results, or situations, tasks, actions, and results. You can also "guide" interviewees with a prompt, such as "Well, you've seen the problem, what action would lead to a favorable result?"

One thing NOT to do: "*You (the interviewer) always want to avoid the use of leading questions. Phrases such as 'I assume that…' or 'Don't you agree that…' clue the applicant how to answer the question appropriately and they will generally respond with what they think you want to hear*" (McKenna, 2004, p. 16).

Evaluation Rubrics and Formats

Rubrics are guides for evaluation and contain criteria and quality indicators. A basic rubric for evaluating candidate answers may have just three levels of evaluation: unacceptable, acceptable, and target. What would be general descriptors for each level of evaluation? What does unacceptable mean? Where is the line between an unacceptable answer and an acceptable one? What would make an answer target?

What Is an Unacceptable Answer?

Unacceptable means that the candidate simply cannot provide an answer to the question. The candidate may say, "I don't know" or he or she may attempt an answer that is simply not correct. Using the premise of BBI, unacceptable answers are ones that indicate that the candidate has had no past experience with the situation or task, or that their past experience was an unsuccessful one.

Example of an unacceptable answer:

Interview question: How have you supplemented the textbook in your classes?

Candidate answer: There is so much mandated by the state and the district guidelines, that it is all we can do to cover the textbook. It would be nice to add some things, but we just don't have the time, and besides, there is never any money for manipulatives or extras.

What Is an Acceptable Answer?

Acceptable means that the candidate has given an answer that meets the minimal level criteria. Acceptable answers show some positive past experience with the situation or task. They show past behavior with a problem that is what you can expect in future performance.

Example of an acceptable answer:

Interview question: How have you supplemented the textbook in your classes?

Candidate answer: The book that I have used for sixth-grade language arts is actually quite good. The book gives ideas for supplemental activities and comes with a CD-ROM that has some fun vocabulary crosswords and enrichment projects. We set up a computer in the corner of the room for students to use the CD-ROM whenever they finish early. They seem to like that and the students who do the CD-ROM seem to score better on their vocabulary quizzes.

What Is a Target Answer?

Target answers wow the interviewer. A target answer goes above and beyond what was expected. They indicate that the candidate has had past positive experiences with the teaching situation and that they can clearly articulate what they have done and will do when hired. Target answers give the interviewer concrete data about whether the candidate has the skills necessary to do the job and if they have had successful experiences in the past.

Example of a target answer:

> Interview question: How have you supplemented the textbook in your classes?

> Candidate answer: The textbook is a big resource for us. It has the readings and vocabulary that are appropriate for sixth-grade level. Before I ever ask the students to read from the book I introduce the topic or theme for a story with a focus activity that I have created. For example, before the students read a story about a girl who had to move, I did a quick survey of who had moved and what it felt like to change towns and schools. I learned that my students had moved a lot more than I have, and they are so young! After the reading, I always try to do a follow-up writing activity. Sometimes this activity involves another subject area, too, if possible. Students need to read, to write, and to draw comparisons between what they are learning in my class and what they might be doing in another class. Of course, I use the textbook supplements too, when appropriate, but mostly I try to add things that make the learning real for my students.

When evaluating answers, it is best to have a copy of the questions in front of each evaluator, with a column for checking unacceptable, acceptable, target. Additionally, there should be a review list at the top of the page of guidelines for unacceptable, acceptable, and target. Before the interviews begin, the interviewer needs an idea of what answers are sought. If a group is interviewing, there must be discussion of what answers are sought, and what would constitute each unacceptable, acceptable, or target rating. Of course, there will always be the issue of reliability among raters. However, with practice, interviewers will become more efficient at determining excellent answers. If 20 questions are used for the interview, it will be easy to tabulate how many answers fall into each column. Clearly, a candidate with the most target answers should be the choice for the job, if all other criteria are met (certification, criminal background check, etc.)

Unacceptable answers:
- no answer provided,
- are incorrect,
- do not demonstrate "best practice" in teaching,
- candidate has no past experience with situation, and
- candidate's past experience was not positive.

Acceptable answers:
- meet the minimal standard,
- show some past positive experience with situation,
- are fairly articulate, and
- give indication that the candidate will be able to perform the action in the future.

Target answers:
- wow the interviewer,
- include articulate, precise vocabulary,
- go above and beyond what might be expected, and
- indicate past positive experience and knowledge of what was learned from the experience.

Using a Numeric Rating Scale

There can be advantages to creating a numeric rating scale for evaluating candidate responses. A rating scale of 1 to 5, 1 to 7, or 1 to 10 may be used. Whatever the numeric scale, the numbers should represent some quality indicators upon which all evaluators have agreed. For example, with a 1 to 5 scale, 1 could indicate a weak answer, 2 a below average answer, 3 an average answer, 4 a fairly strong answer, and 5 a very strong answer.

Table 5.1. Sample Numeric Rating Scale 1 to 5				
Weak Answer	Below Average	Average Answer	Fairly Strong Answer	Very Strong
1	2	3	4	5
1. How do you begin a lesson?	1　2　3　4　5			
2. Tell us about typical homework assignments that you have given.	1　2　3　4　5			
3. What kinds of classroom management plans have you implemented in the past?	1　2　3　4　5			
4. How have you communicated with your students' parents?	1　2　3　4　5			
5. How have you promoted acceptance, tolerance, and cultural diversity in your classes?	1　2　3　4　5			

For a numeric rating scale of 1 to 7, 1 might be used to indicate no past experience with the situation or task, 2 would indicate limited experience, 3 would indicate some experience, and 4 would indicate an average level of previous positive experience with the situation or task. A 5 on this scale would indicate that the candidate had past experience and could articulate his or her experience in an above average manner, 6 could indicate significant experience and a well above average ability to articulate learning from the experience, and 7 would indicate much experience and an excellent ability to talk about teaching experiences (see Table 5.2).

When the candidate is talking about past teaching experiences, the evaluator should attempt to discern what was learned from the experience as a way to predict the skills the candidate will bring to the new job. The numbers would appear at the top of the rating form, as well as beside the questions.

Using a scale of 1 to 10 gives further room to differentiate answers. However, most evaluators will look at a scale of 1 to 10 and see percentages, then think of grades that go with the percentages. For example, in the world of schooling, 60% is the minimal cutoff for a D-, or a passing grade. Seventy percent may be the lowest cut for a C, average, and 80% for a B. Ninety percent traditionally marks the lowest A, and 100% is perfect.

If using a 1 to 10 scale for an evaluation instrument, thought might be given to just having the scale be 1, and then 6 through 10. This way, 1 indicates an unacceptable answer, 6 indicates a minimally acceptable answer, 7 an average answer, 8 a good answer, 9 a very good answer, and 10 a perfect or "target" answer (see Table 5.3).

Table 5.2. Sample Numeric Rating Scale 1 to 7

For each of the following questions, rate the candidate's past experience with the situation or task, and the candidate's ability to articulate what was learned from the experience as a way to predict the skills that they will bring to the new position.

No Experience	Limited	Some	Average	Above Average	Well Above	Excellent
1	2	3	4	5	6	7

1. Give an example of a state or national curriculum standard and how you have taught to that standard in a lesson.	1	2	3	4	5	6	7
2. What is a current trend in this grade/subject field and how have you dealt with/ incorporated this trend?	1	2	3	4	5	6	7
3. What stress factors have you seen in students at this grade level and how have you helped the students cope with stress?	1	2	3	4	5	6	7
4. How have you encouraged and met the needs of gifted, talented, and advanced students in your classes?	1	2	3	4	5	6	7
5. How have you kept your principal or department chair informed of class activities and successes?	1	2	3	4	5	6	7

Table 5.3. Sample Numeric Rating Scale 1 to 10					
Unacceptable	Minimally Acceptable	Average	Good	Very Good	On Target
1	6	7	8	9	10
1. Explain your grading scale as though you were explaining it to students the first week of class.	1 6 7 8 9 10				
2. How have you communicated standardized test scores to students and parents?	1 6 7 8 9 10				
3. How have you integrated technology into your classes?	1 6 7 8 9 10				
4. Describe a personal problem that a student brought to you and how you handled the situation.	1 6 7 8 9 10				
5. Describe a lesson where you integrated a social skill into an academic lesson. (Elementary education)	1 6 7 8 9 10				

Other Assessment Instruments

James Stronge (2002) suggests the use of assessment checklists, based on indicators of the qualities of effective teachers. For example, if a quality deemed important for a teacher is caring, Stronge suggests that two indicators of that quality would be "Exhibits active listening" and "Shows concern for students' emotional and physical well-being" (2002, p. 71). The rating of the teacher for those two indicators would be: not observed, ineffective, apprentice, professional, and master (see Table 5.4). If this type of checklist were used for evaluating interview questions, then the interviewer would ask a question and rate the answer based on how ineffective, apprentice, professional, and master teachers might answer it. Of course, the names indicating the experience of the teacher could be changed to make the checklist fit the interview format.

In the following example, the ineffective teacher is one whose answer indicates no experience with the question, or whose answer does not indicate accepted best practice (i.e., teacher says she yells to get the class' attention and to make transitions). The new teacher is characterized as one whose answers indicate some training and limited experience; this person meets minimal guidelines. A professional teacher is generally one with more than 2 years of experience and who can articulate past experiences with evidence that he or she has learned and grown from both coursework and practice. A master teacher is the one that everyone wants teaching his or her children. The master teacher has the proverbial "withitness" and is able to engage and motivate students to high levels of achievement.

It should be noted that creating a rating scale with the divisions of ineffective, new teacher (novice), professional, and master, in no way means that new teachers are not professional in their work, or that only veteran, experienced teachers should be hired. In fact, it has often been said that "practice doesn't make perfect, but it does make permanent." Having taught lessons in a poor manner for many years does not make an exemplary teacher. This rating system just gives evaluators another option of assessing answers.

It would be great if all candidates were indeed proven master teachers, who had not burned out over the course of learning their trade. However, this is not the case and employers will be hiring new

Table 5.4. Sample Assessment Without Numeric Rating			
Ineffective Teacher I	New Teacher N	Professional Teacher P	Master Teacher M
1. Describe a lesson you have taught that combined auditory, visual, and/or kinesthetic teaching strategies.	I	N	P M
2. Describe a topic considered hard to teach in your field, and a lesson that you have used to engage students on this topic.	I	N	P M
3. Describe modifications that you have made to an assignment so that a student could master the material successfully in spite of an exceptionality.	I	N	P M
4. Describe a lesson where you used higher-order questions to challenge students.	I	N	P M
5. How have you set up a classroom to facilitate "time on task?"	I	N	P M

teachers with a variety of experiences and training. There is not one right model for establishing an evaluation model for interviews, just as there is not one right model that fits all teaching situations. Once a model is chosen, it is then time to put the pieces of the puzzle together and combine BBI questions with an evaluation model to create the interview format.

Chapter 6
Preliminary Interview Formats With Behavior-Based Interviewing

Telephone and job fair interviews are two preliminary interview formats. BBI can streamline these interviews, providing usable data for sorting large numbers of candidates. Additionally, preliminary interviews can be an opportune time to further "sell" your district.

How Preliminary Interviews Relate to Retention

Preliminary interviews provide a way to give the "realistic job preview" (RJP) that businesses have found so helpful. Research conducted by Edward Liu as part of Harvard's *Project on the Next Generation of New Teachers* has shown that the more information a candidate receives about a potential job from the employer during the interview process, the more likely the candidate is to be satisfied when hired. Therefore, an "information-rich" job preview, where employers not only ask questions but provide information, may help the candidate to understand the position better, and have expectations met (Johnson, et al., 2005). A strong preliminary interview may provide such information—and a candidate feels "wooed" by the employer if he or she wins a later interview based on the preliminary one.

The Telephone Interview

A thorough sort of application materials may yield more candidates than need to be interviewed on-site. If a significant amount of time has elapsed between the initial job advertisement and the sorting of candidates, phone interviews should be used to ascertain which candidates are actively job searching and are still interested in the position. A second purpose of the phone interview is to determine certification status of seniors who applied before graduation, while their certification status was incomplete. The applicant should be asked if his or her references can be contacted, if this permission was not clarified on application materials. Lastly, the telephone interview can be a key component of the sorting process.

Before a candidate is called, the employer should create a master list of questions, both of administrative questions, and those which will have value for sorting, ranking, and selection of candidates. It is important to start a telephone interview with a clear introduction of the caller, and why the call is being made. If an interviewer wishes to record the call, that must be stated immediately, and the candidate must give permission for the conversation to be recorded. Also, since candidates have no advance notice of a call, employers should ask if the timing of the call is a convenient one, or if a better time exists later that same day. Since many students only have cell phones, it is unreasonable to expect that they continue the phone interview while driving in heavy traffic!

Some candidates may send a very strong cover letter and resume, but may not have completed your required district paperwork, perhaps not sending in the district application, criminal background check, or transcripts. Failure to complete all paperwork in a timely manner may indicate that the candidate will be tardy with paperwork in the future, since past behavior is the best predictor of future performance. However, if a very strong candidate in a high-needs field is missing paperwork, then a quick call from an employer, or office support staff person, can be used to ask if they still intend to be a candidate, and if so, giving them of a new deadline for required materials. This may be considered part of recruiting the candidate.

As you develop the questions that you want for your telephone interview, write them on a form with an assessment rubric or numeric scale. Ten questions may be far too many for a 20-minute telephone interview, so you may want to limit your questions to administrative questions and three to five sorting questions.

To end the phone interview, it is important to thank the candidate for his or her time, and to let them know how and when they will hear the result of the phone interview. Many employers end the conversation stating, "We will be making calls to several candidates over the next few days. We will make follow-up calls next week to invite candidates for on-site interviews and will mail letters to all candidates regarding the status of applications at the end of next week. If you have a question, you may call or email (insert staff member) after (insert date), but nothing will be decided before that date." It is critical that interviewers not sound overly optimistic to any candidates at this point. Some candidates might think that an optimistic phone conversation means a certain interview, or even a future job offer. Allow plenty of time before establishing a deadline when candidates may call with questions, because they will call if that option is open to them.

Table 6.1. Sample Questions for the Telephone Interview

Administrative Questions

- After an introduction of the caller, ask if this is a convenient time to speak for x-number of minutes. Explain the nature of the call—administrative questions only, or preliminary interview questions.
- You have an application on file with our office. Are you still interested in the position, and, if so, why?
- May we contact the references listed on your application?
- Your application states that you will be certified pending graduation and a passing score on the state certification test. Have you now graduated and passed the test?

Ten Sample Sorting Questions

- Tell me about the best teaching experience you have had.
- Name one accomplishment from your previous teaching that characterizes your work.
- How much experience have you had with this grade/subject level?
- Describe a typical lesson that you have taught.
- In your cover letter, you mention _____. Describe what you learned from that experience.
- Describe a problem that you have encountered in motivating students to accomplish academically, and what you have learned to overcome that problem.
- Describe a classroom where you have taught, in terms of how it was organized.
- Tell me about a positive classroom management experience that you have had.
- What parts of your teacher education program do you use the most?
- What else would you like to tell me about yourself with regard to your teaching experience?

Calling to Arrange an Interview

Calling is a convenient way to extend the invitation to interview. Creating a checklist will ensure that the staff member who makes the call covers all the necessary information in a timely manner. Important information to convey includes:

- Identify who is calling and the reason for the call.
- Verify that the person called is the candidate and that he or she is still interested in the position.

Then explain:

- when the interview is to be scheduled,
- who will conduct the interview (one person or a group),
- the length of the interview,
- whether or not the interview will be recorded, and if so, for whom,
- any special materials needed for the interview (video of a class taught, a short lesson to be taught, portfolio, proof of citizenship/eligibility to work, any other paperwork),
- complete directions to the school/interview site and parking options,
- how to contact the staff member for future questions/how to cancel the interview, and
- some more information about the district and how interested the district is in hiring the strongest candidates (remember the need to "recruit" and "woo" candidates).

Whenever possible, avoid leaving messages with parents, children, or roommates. Messages can certainly be left on answering machines, but remember that those messages can get lost. Email has become a viable option for contacting candidates.

Use of Email Instead of Calling

Many people would like electronic mail to completely replace paper mail and telephone use. The district may want to use email for asking candidates administrative questions about their interest in the position, and completion of paperwork, graduation, and state testing. You may want to select the questions you would use for a phone interview and email them to candidates as a preliminary interview. Give the candidates a deadline to respond via email, and let candidates know that these questions are being evaluated for decisions regarding who will be invited to on-site interviews. Remember, however, that when this medium is used, candidates can, and probably will, get help from others to answer your questions.

Email can be used to alert candidates that you will be calling within the next 2 weeks, and sample questions for the phone interview can be shared. For this email message, you would NOT want candidates to send you responses to the questions, but rather the candidates would receive a pool of questions, knowing that some will be asked when they receive the telephone interview call.

Email has many advantages. Busy students who are difficult to catch with a phone call often check their email throughout the day. Email can create a permanent record; it is written, traceable, and can be archived. The employer can read the email and also gain insight from it about the candidate's writing skills, which are important skills for teachers.

The disadvantage of email is that is does not give the interviewer any verbal cues. Some students write beautifully, but cannot maintain eye contact or express themselves clearly when talking. Good verbal communication is tremendously important for teachers. Email is not secure or confidential; grades and test scores should not be transmitted via email. Many practicing teachers currently use email to communicate with parents, instead of the traditional method of sending notes home.

Many administrators find that giving an email address to candidates instead of a phone number is a viable way to answer candidate questions when their time permits, without the interruption of phone calls. An even better idea is to give the email address of a support staff person, requesting that no calls be made, but that questions will be answered via email. Of course, that support staff person should respond to emails in a timely manner. How the district responds to calls and messages is part of the overall recruitment process. Today's candidates want to feel recruited, and may make their decision about which job offer to accept based on how they are treated during the pre-interview and interview process.

The medium of email has grown exponentially, and may quickly replace calling as a means of communication between employers and job candidates. Some businesses accept resumes only electronically, and some districts expect their candidates to use existing state online databases to register for job openings. Again, confidentiality is always an issue when email and online mediums are used. Extra care should be given when considering what information will be sent electronically.

Job Fair Preliminary Interviews

Job fairs provide opportunities to meet a large number of potential candidates in a short amount of time. More than in the past, districts use fairs to recruit students to apply for positions in their schools, luring them with competitive salaries, special benefits, and DVDs that showcase their communities. This is indeed time to share information and provide realistic job previews with potential hires. Some job fairs provide time for recruiters to conduct short interviews with the candidates. The interview questions for job fairs can be structured much like the ones of the telephone or email interview, with the advantage that the interviewer will get to watch the candidate answer, and will be able to gain some insight from the non-verbal cues. Enthusiasm, poise, eye contact, and posture tell quite a bit about a person.

You will want to create a checklist for job fair candidates. From each candidate you will need the following:

- resume,
- complete name, contact information, and certification area, if not on resume,
- specifics of certification area/certification completion date/availability to start, and
- interests in special areas (coaching a sport, student council, honor society sponsor, tutoring, etc.)

Then, add a list of questions that you will ask, with a simple assessment rubric or numeric evaluation.

- Tell me about your experience teaching this grade and/or subject area.
- Name one accomplishment from your previous teaching that characterizes your work.
- If I had walked into your classroom in the past, describe what I would have seen.
- Describe the components of a good lesson. How do you know it was a good one?

- Tell me about a challenge or problem from your previous classroom experience that you resolved.

Lastly—you need to make sure candidates leave a job fair interview with your district application, contact information, and some "facts and figures" about the district. A pen, a CD-ROM with district highlights, or even a piece of candy is a nice touch, too, since everyone loves a free gift. As Roling and Vanderwall (2000) write, "...today's job market calls for new approaches and proactive strategies. Take the initiative to pursue those candidates of most interest to you!" (p. 14). Some recruiters take prolific notes and evaluate with a checklist or scoring system while interviewing at job fairs, even for 10-minute interviews. Others may make a quick judgement as the candidate leaves to put the paperwork in a "target" file, "maybe" file, or "non-matches" file.

After returning to the office, reviewing the paperwork, and including required applications sent in from screened candidates at the fair, the employer can select top candidates and contact them for on-site interviews.

Remember to "sell" the challenges and family friendliness of the teaching profession in preliminary and on-site interviews.

"What employees want today is not what they have wanted in the past. Sure, the needs of food, shelter, and safety are prerequisites. Beyond that, what today's employees want is a challenge, an opportunity to grow, rewards for work done well and recognition of their worth as individuals. They want to be able to try different jobs, not necessarily higher-ranking ones, so that they can expand their knowledge.

They want to be appreciated for who they are, as an individual, not just as an employee. They want employers to recognize that to them life is more than work—that family and playtime are also important. The companies that can meet these needs will be the ones who succeed and continue to succeed" (Haggerty, 2001).

Table 6.2. Telephone Interview Worksheet

Position sought: _____

Date and time of call: _____

Candidate's name: _____

Phone number: _____

1. Introduction of the caller. Is this a convenient time?
2. You have an application on file with our office. Are you still interested in the position, and, if so, why?
3. What is your status regarding earned certification at this time?
4. May we contact the references you have listed on your application?

Questions	Unacceptable	Acceptable	Target
1. Tell me about the best teaching experience you have had.	U	A	T
2. Name one accomplishment from your previous teaching that characterizes your work.	U	A	T
3. How much experience have you had with this grade/subject level?	U	A	T
4. Describe a typical lesson that you have taught.	U	A	T
5. Tell me about a positive classroom management experience that you have had.	U	A	T

We will be calling candidates through _____. All candidates will receive a letter or email about their status by _____. You may contact our district after _____ at the following addresses or numbers:

Thank you so much for your time and interest in our district.

Table 6.3. Job Fair Interview Checklist

Collect from each candidate:

_____ 1. Resume

_____ 2. Complete name, contact information, and certification area, if not on resume.

Ask for information:

3. Tell me the specifics of your certification area. When will your certification be complete and when are you available to start?

4. Do you have any interest in special areas? If so, which ones? (coaching a sport, student council, honor society sponsor, tutoring, etc.)

Questions:	Unacceptable	Acceptable	Target
1. Tell me about your experience teaching this grade and/or subject area.	U	A	T
2. Name one accomplishment from your previous teaching that characterizes your work.	U	A	T
3. If I had walked into your classroom in the past, describe what I would have seen.	U	A	T
4. Describe the components of a good lesson. How do you know it was a good one?	U	A	T
5. Tell me about a challenge or problem from your previous classroom experience that you resolved.	U	A	T

Table 6.3. Job Fair Interview Checklist *(continued)*

Overall comments:

Appropriate dress?

Enthusiasm?

Interpersonal skills?

Reminders to self about candidate:

Does the candidate have:

_____ 1. District application

_____ 2. Contact information

_____ 3. District facts and figures CD-ROM or handout

_____ 4. A sense of being recruited and wooed?

Chapter 7

On-Site Behavior-Based Interviewing Interviews

The on-site interview remains the most popular means of meeting and sorting candidates. An in-person interview provides the employer with verbal and non-verbal cues. In actuality, the interviewer gets to see how candidates present themselves, and those who do so well, can probably present themselves equally well to students, parents, colleagues, and other administrators. Since much of teaching is communicating, the interview gives the candidates the opportunity to "teach" about themselves. A candidate who provides clear, concise answers should be able to give clear, concise answers to student questions in class. A candidate who is nervous about talking to one or two interviewers may be quite nervous when facing 25 students in a class. A candidate who smiles, appears composed, and even indicates a sense of humor, will bring those positive traits to the classroom.

The interview is also a recruitment tool. Today's candidates want to feel that they are being recruited into a good school system where they can make a difference. Including a school tour, a meeting with other teachers, and "selling" the school during the interview are all part of recruitment. If the school is "high-needs" with many at-risk students, a savvy administrator can appeal to the candidate's sense of mission. Information-rich job interviews that accurately preview the job will enable new teachers to feel that there were "no surprises."

When supported in the new job—and when there are few, if any, negative surprises—a new hire's expectations are met and that hire is more apt to be retained in the district.

"Beyond the basics of where and what he will teach, the more information the teacher candidate can gather, the more he understands the challenges the job will present and the supports that the workplace will offer" (Johnson, et al. 2005, p. 30).

The Importance of Clarity of Expectations

While the interview is the time to sort candidates and decide on the strongest match between the job and the new teacher, it is also a time to make expectations of the position crystal clear. It will not be possible to retain new hires who say, "This is not at all what I expected." Whenever possible, interview for a specific position—second-grade teacher, seventh-grade language arts, or 10th-grade English. Within the advertised job, be as specific as possible, such as "10th-grade English, with six classes a day, three of which will be lower-level, general classes." If the position is not yet fully determined, such as high school sections for the new teacher, be clear about how and when the final assignment will be made.

Alerting the new teacher that he or she will be accepting a position for "general English teacher, up to six classes a day in the field, any grade 9-12" is a must if the assignment simply can't be made by interview time. In elementary schools, teachers are often very adamant about which grade they want, and hiring a teacher for a third-grade position, then informing that teacher that he or she will actually be in fifth-grade can prove catastrophic (and may lead to a union battle in some areas). Above all, practice "truth in advertising" as described in Chapter 1, both in advertising the position and in selling the position in the interview.

Flexibility is a good trait for a teacher to have. If your staffing needs are such that teachers will be moved frequently over the next 3 years, and a candidate indicates displeasure with that, it may be a red flag that he or she doesn't have the flexibility needed to work in your school. Again, the important thing is that everyone involved—the employer, the candidate, and the veteran teachers on staff, know the expectations ahead of time. Veteran teachers may not be happy if the new hire appears to get all of the best students for a grade level, or gets a lighter load.

Who Will Interview?

There are as many formulas for who is involved in hiring as there are school districts. Personnel directors may conduct job fair interviews, using central office staff to help sort paperwork. Some personnel directors then send three to six candidate files to the principal of the school with openings and the principal conducts on-site interviews with three from that pool. Some principals know their schools' student teachers and want to interview them as finalists, as well as other teachers they know to be job searching. Principals then make sure that the potential candidates apply through the central office and personnel director. A personnel director can be very helpful in finding glitches in certification of which the principal was not aware.

The size of the school district is often a major determinant of how hiring is handled and who does final interviews. Some large schools have the curriculum director or assistant principal serve as the on-site contact for applicants, and he or she conducts interviews, then presents final candidates to the principal for a cursory 10-minute interview and approval. Interviewing by committee is becoming more and more popular in schools with site-based management.

No matter the process and the people involved, the process must be transparent to all. In fact, post the hiring process in each school office and faculty lounge, if it is not already clear. If the teachers' union is involved, and hiring practices are included in the contract, make sure that everyone is aware of the contractual guidelines, and uses them. Take a moment and write out the hiring process for your school/district and indicate the person responsible for each step (see Table 7.1).

Training of Interviewers

With decisions made about who does what, a training component must be added to the formula. Perhaps the personnel director will share copies of this book with all administrators involved in the hiring process, and then have a meeting to go over the guidelines. A superintendent or director of professional/staff development can offer an inservice program for all involved in the hiring process. Support staff and secretaries who will meet the candidates need sufficient training about guidelines and illegal questions. Teachers need to be informed that positions are advertised and that candidates may be seen taking tours of the building. Teachers involved on hiring committees need training seminars. Included in the training should be time for the interviewers to create their master list of specific BBI questions that will be used for each interview.

Table 7.1. Hiring Guidelines and Persons Designated
1. Advertisement of position.
2. Attends recruitment fairs.
3. Gathers all paperwork for candidates.
4. Informs candidates of district paperwork that is due/answers phone and email inquiries.
5. Phone interviews.
6. Selects finalists for on-site interviews.
7. Contacts and makes arrangements for on-site interviews (including parking, travel reimbursements, overnight accommodations, etc.).
8. Conducts on-site interviews.
9. Makes final decision for recommendation of new hire to administration/board.
10. Informs candidate of hiring decisions/starts induction process and paperwork.

Illegal Questions

It remains illegal to ask any questions of candidates regarding their gender, race, color, national origin, religion, age, or disabilities. As one looks at the fine points of these categories, the interviewer cannot ask about marital status, children, or where someone lives. An interviewer cannot comment on a candidate's dress or jewelry, as that might be indicative of national origin. For example, commenting on a pretty diamond ring on a woman's hand might indicate that the interviewer is asking about marital status. Saying, "What a pretty ring— tell me about it" is illegal in an interview.

Many schools have found that keeping a list of illegal question topics in front of the interviewers is a good idea. It is also important to provide the same guidelines to the support and secretarial staff. Often, a well-meaning support staff member may strike up a conversation with a candidate who is waiting for an interview. Questions as simple as, "Haven't I seen you at my church?", or "Is our weather different than from where you grew up?" are out of line. Again, commenting on jewelry and clothes is inappropriate, as a simple piece of jewelry may be indicative of religion, ethnicity, or sexual preference. See the reminder sheet on Table 7.2 (Green, 1996; Kaplan, 2002).

Arranging Interviews

With a set of questions prepared, an evaluation system determined, paperwork sorted, and preliminary interviews completed, it is time to conduct the on-site interviews. How should you plan for the most productive interviews? Time is of the essence. Interviews should not be interrupted by students, teachers, phone calls, or beepers. A candidate who is searching for a supportive work environment might say, "if the administrator didn't have time for me during my arranged interview, how much consideration will he or she have for me as an employee?" Many administrators admit that they can determine much about a candidate in one hour. Some districts allow 45 minutes with each administrator and/or group interview, making for a much longer interview. Decide in advance how much time will be spent and adhere to a schedule. Preferably, candidates shouldn't bump into each other in the office or parking lot, either, since many times candidates will know each other.

Pre-interview arrangements can be made by the interviewer or a staff person, but should be clearly made in advance. The invitation to

Table 7.2. Illegal Question Reminders

No questions or comments may be made about:

- Gender—or gender preferences, roommates, living arrangements
- Race
- National origin—How long have you lived here? Where are you from originally? What is your native language?
- Religion
- Age—What year did you graduate from high school?
- Disabilities—including personal questions about height and weight
- Arrest record (conviction record may be checked)
- Were you honorably discharged from the military?
- You may NOT ask questions or make comments about: (not even innocent, "small talk" questions)

Children	Marriage
Smoking	Jewelry
Clothing	Spouse's work

Affiliations (social clubs, organizations)

interview, when handled well, is a recruitment tool. Few districts reimburse candidates for mileage or overnight accommodations, but be prepared for that question when candidates are invited to interview. Be clear about everything from parking to which door to use when entering the building.

Getting the Interview Off to a Good Start

Of course, shaking hands is a must. Even before the handshake, it is good to walk out of your office to greet the candidate, indicate where to sit, and begin with a warm, friendly tone. Thanking the candidate is appropriate at the beginning and end of an interview.

Be sure to tell the candidate that you will be taking notes and referring to some pre-set questions. If you are videotaping or making an audiotape that should have been discussed in the interview invitation phone call, but should also be mentioned again at this time. Videotapes can be a good way to send candidates' interviews on to principals. There should be a deadline for when the tape will be erased, as well.

Go through your questions, making notes, checking marks, or circling ratings. Be sure to ask if the applicant has questions of you. If you are unable to explain salary and benefits, make sure that the applicant can spend a few minutes with someone who can. Make sure you inform all candidates of the hiring timeline, when candidates will be notified, and how to contact the employer if they need to.

Importance of Candidate's Questions

The candidate's questions are important for two reasons. First, the candidate's questions may indicate whether or not he or she has prepared for the interview. Asking a very simple question about salary, school size, or school history may indicate that the candidate didn't even read the district's Web site before the interview. However, when a candidate is prepared, a question from him or her may indicate genuine interest, such as, "I read on your Web site that the school celebrated its 50th anniversary in this building and that there is now a mini museum on the third floor. Can I see it?" Some positive questions from candidates include:

- Tell me more about your mentoring program.

- You indicated that your district provides ongoing professional development. What opportunities might be available for me next year?
- Please tell me more about the technology available in classrooms.
- How would you describe the parent involvement in this school?
- In what ways are teachers involved in site-based management decisions?

The second reason to ask candidates for their questions is because you may have inadvertently forgotten something very important. When a candidate is genuinely interested in a job, he or she will want to know about class size, where the classroom is, if the room is shared, and when decisions about the position will be made. A strong candidate may have had a wonderful experience that one of your questions didn't address. Let them share that experience in this part of the interview. In fact, some employers ask, "Do you have any questions for me?" and "Is there anything else that you want to tell me about your past teaching experience that you haven't yet had a chance to share? A good interview is also a good conversation—and conversations are two-way in nature.

End the interview in a timely manner. Again, common courtesy is important—walking a candidate out of your office, shaking hands, etc. If you are in a large office building or school, make sure they know how to find the parking lot again. Sometimes, student workers can walk a candidate out to their car, provided that student workers have had some training in what to say and not say to candidates. Everyone that meets the candidate is part of the on-site interview process and part of the recruitment process.

Table 7.3. Sample On-Site Interview for a Second-Grade Position

Candidate name: _____

Position: _____

Date: _____ Start time: _____ End time: _____

Reminders:

1. We will be talking for about _____.
   Then you will meet with _____.

2. I will refer to my questions and will be taking notes.

3. Other:

U = Unacceptable   A = Acceptable   T = Target

Opening:

1. You indicated on your resume that you have been involved with _____. Please tell me more about that.	U	A	T

Curriculum:

2. Tell me about your experiences teaching the second-grade curriculum. Specifically, what are the most important topics/goals for this grade?	U	A	T
3. Describe your experiences teaching reading.	U	A	T

Planning/Methods:

4. What are some of your tried-and-true ways to start and end a lesson?	U	A	T
5. How have you used manipulatives or activities to teach a lesson?	U	A	T

Assessment:

6. Tell me about how you have prepared students for standardized tests.	U	A	T
7. Describe a grading scale or anecdotal records for second-graders.	U	A	T

Table 7.3. Sample On-Site Interview for a Second-Grade Position (continued)

Classroom Management:

8. Describe your movement in a classroom on a typical morning.   U   A   T

9. Describe a successful management plan that you have used.   U   A   T

10. Tell me about a time when a student was confrontational or misbehaving. What did you do?   U   A   T

Communication/Peers:

11. Describe your experiences planning with other teachers.   U   A   T

12. Describe a good parent communication that you have used (letter, call, or in-person).   U   A   T

Meeting Student Needs/Special Needs:

13. Describe an at-risk student with whom you have worked and what you did for that student.   U   A   T

Professionalism:

14. Describe a time when you knew that you had achieved success with students.   U   A   T

15. What are you reading to stay current in your field?   U   A   T

Check when done:

Describe assignment (size, room, etc.)   _____

Describe salary/benefits   _____

Informed candidate of hiring timeline   _____

Candidate knows who to contact if…   _____

What other questions do you have for me at this time?

Is there anything else that you would like to share about your past experience or qualifications?

Table 7.4. Sample On-Site Interview for a Fifth-Grade Position

Candidate name: _____

Position: _____

Date: _____ Start time: _____ End time: _____

Reminders:

1. We will be talking for about _____.
   Then you will meet with _____.
2. I will refer to my questions and will be taking notes.
3. Other:

U = Unacceptable   A = Acceptable   T = Target

Opening:

1. You indicated on your resume that you have been   U   A   T
   involved with _____.
   Please tell me more about that.

Curriculum:

2. Tell me about your experiences teaching the fifth-   U   A   T
   grade curriculum. Specifically, what are the most
   important topics/goals for this grade?

3. Describe your experiences teaching social studies   U   A   T
   and math in the age group.

Planning/Methods:

4. What are some of your tried-and-true ways to start   U   A   T
   and end a lesson?

5. How have you used activities or projects to teach   U   A   T
   a lesson?

Assessment:

6. Tell me about how you have prepared students for   U   A   T
   standardized tests.

7. Describe a grading scale for fifth-graders.   U   A   T

Table 7.4. Sample On-Site Interview for a Fifth-Grade Position *(continued)*

Classroom Management:

8. Describe your movement in a classroom on a typical morning.   U   A   T

9. Describe a successful management plan that you have used.   U   A   T

10. Tell me about a time when a student was confrontational or misbehaving. What did you do?   U   A   T

Communication/Peers:

11. Describe your experiences planning with other teachers.   U   A   T

12. Describe a good parent communication that you have used (letter, call, or in-person).   U   A   T

Meeting Student Needs/Special Needs:

13. Describe an at-risk student with whom you have worked and what you did for that student.   U   A   T

14. Describe a typical fifth-grader and his or her developmental needs   U   A   T

Professionalism:

15. Describe a time when you knew that you had achieved success with students.   U   A   T

16. What are you reading to stay current in your field?   U   A   T

Check when done:

Describe assignment (size, room, etc.)   _____

Describe salary/benefits   _____

Informed candidate of hiring timeline   _____

Candidate knows who to contact if…   _____

What other questions do you have for me at this time?

Is there anything else that you would like to share about your past experience or qualifications?

Table 7.5. Sample On-Site Interview for a Seventh-Grade Mathematics Position

Candidate name: _____

Position: _____

Date: _____ Start time: _____ End time: _____

Reminders:

1. We will be talking for about _____.
   Then you will meet with _____.

2. I will refer to my questions and will be taking notes.

3. Other:

U = Unacceptable   A = Acceptable   T = Target

Opening:

1. You indicated on your resume that you have been involved with _____.
   Please tell me more about that.   U A T

Uniqueness of Middle School Concept/Students:

2. Tell me about when you have worked on a teaching team or in a "school within a school" setting.   U A T

3. Describe a typical seventh-grader and his or her needs.   U A T

Curriculum:

4. Which mathematics skills are most crucial for this grade and why?   U A T

5. How have you worked with other teachers to integrate mathematics into their courses?   U A T

6. The improvement of students' reading skills is important during middle school. Tell me about your experiences with reading or writing, either directly teaching them or integrating them into mathematics.   U A T

Planning/Methods:

7. Describe a successful lesson that you have taught that helped your students learn the material.   U A T

8. Describe teaching strategies that help students prepare for standardized tests.   U A T

Table 7.5. Sample On-Site Interview for a Seventh-Grade Mathematics Position *(continued)*			

Classroom Management/Climate:

9. What have you implemented to make your classroom welcoming and "student friendly"?   U A T

10. Describe a management plan that you have used, including rules and corrective actions.   U A T

11. What words or phrases have become typical positive reinforcements in your teaching vocabulary? How do middle school students respond to this type of reinforcement?   U A T

12. Describe a confrontation you have had with a student and how it was resolved.   U A T

Special Needs:

13. Middle school students can be quite "clique-ish." How have you promoted acceptance and tolerance in your classroom?   U A T

14. What modifications have you used to help special needs students succeed?   U A T

Communication/Professionalism:

15. Describe positive parent communications that you have used in the past   U A T

16. How do you stay current with trends and issues in middle grades education?   U A T

Check when done:

Describe assignment (size, room, etc.)   _____

Describe salary/benefits   _____

Informed candidate of hiring timeline   _____

Candidate knows who to contact if…   _____

What other questions do you have for me at this time?

Is there anything else that you would like to share about your past experience or qualifications?

Table 7.6. Sample On-Site Interview for a High School History Position

Candidate name: _____

Position: _____

Date: _____ Start time: _____ End time: _____

Reminders:

1. We will be talking for about _____.
   Then you will meet with _____.
2. I will refer to my questions and will be taking notes.
3. Other:

U = Unacceptable   A = Acceptable   T = Target

Opening:

1. You indicated on your resume that you have been   U   A   T
   involved with _____.
   Please tell me more about that.

Curriculum:

2. Tell me how you interest students in learning Amer-   U   A   T
   ican history.

3. Give an example of a national or state standard in   U   A   T
   history and how you have taught a lesson incorpo-
   rating that standard.

4. How have you supplemented the textbook in his-   U   A   T
   tory classes?

Planning/Methods:

5. Describe the steps of teaching a high school class   U   A   T
   for a 55-minute period.

6. Which methods do you most frequently employ in   U   A   T
   teaching?

7. Describe any projects or group work that have been   U   A   T
   successful with students.

8. How have you prepared students for standardized   U   A   T
   tests and/or graduation tests?

Student Motivation:

9. How have you encouraged students to stay in   U   A   T
   school and graduate?

Table 7.6. Sample On-Site Interview for a High School History Position *(continued)*

10. What kinds of stressors do today's teens face and how have you helped them to cope with their concerns?	U	A	T
11. How have you met the needs of gifted, talented, and advanced students in your classes?	U	A	T
12. How have you helped at-risk students to achieve academic success in your classes?	U	A	T

Assessment and Management:

13. Explain your grading scale to me as though you were explaining it to your 10th-grade class.	U	A	T
14. Explain your classroom management plan to me as though you were explaining it to ninth-graders.	U	A	T
15. Describe a time when your authority, or a class rule, was broken and how you reacted.	U	A	T

Communication/Professionalism:

16. How have you communicated long-range plans to students and parents?	U	A	T
17. How have you supported students' participation or become better acquainted with them through their extracurricular activities?	U	A	T
18. How do you stay current in your subject matter field and in the field of teaching?	U	A	T

Check when done:

Describe assignment (size, room, etc.)   _____

Describe salary/benefits   _____

Informed candidate of hiring timeline   _____

Candidate knows who to contact if…   _____

What other questions do you have for me at this time?

Is there anything else that you would like to share about your past experience or qualifications?

Scenarios for Discussion—On-Site Interviews

1. A recent college graduate arrives for the interview well-dressed and on time. Her paperwork was well done and her grades are quite good. After the third interview question, the candidate breaks down into tears for no apparent reason. Once the tears begin, she says, "I'm so sorry. I just want this job so badly and I am so scared about this interview." What is your reaction to this candidate? Will you continue the interview?

2. After asking four or five questions, it has become apparent that the candidate has quite an attitude. He has made declarations such as, "I won't have discipline problems. I just won't because I'm a 35-year old male teaching middle school." He has indicated that he will coach, but only on his terms; he won't need a mentor, and please don't ask him to do any of the dumb "warm and fuzzy" planning and committee activities with other teachers. He can run his own show. In his own words, "Give me a class and let me teach." Twenty minutes of your planned one-hour interview are over. Do you continue? Do you consider him?

3. You are interviewing for a general science teacher. The assignment will most probably be six general classes a day of required life sciences. A candidate who has applied for this position is quite strong, and can also teach upper level mathematics. As the interview ends, the candidate asks, "Is this assignment set in stone? I mean, I would love to work here in your school, but I will need some upper level classes if you want me to agree to a contract." What can you do? How much flexibility do you have?

4. A candidate arrives at the interview with her 4-year old child. She apologizes in advance, stating that the child's babysitter had to go to the hospital and no one else was available, but reassures you that her child will play quietly in the corner. The child does indeed play quietly and the interview is very strong. Does this influence your decision? What are the positives learned here? Are there any red flags?

5. You have just asked a candidate for a high school history position this question, "What kinds of stressors do today's teens face and how have you helped them to cope with their concerns?" Her response is, "I have been trained to teach all areas of history. My job is academic; it's not to be the counselor or psychologist. My room will be academic and I will work hard so that the students will have high passing rates on the state exams. One thing that I would like to change about schools is that I think we should make them places of academic excellence again, not babysitting and counseling services." How do you rate this answer?

Chapter 8
Final Decisions and Negotiations

Some employers say that they "just know" when a candidate is the right one for the job. However, Deems (1994) reminds interviewers that the final decision to hire should be based on more than "a gut feeling." Some people may interview well but not be able to manage a class and some may not be as poised and polished in an interview but will be able to teach third-graders beautifully. Since BBI is built on the premise of asking about specific teaching knowledge, procedures, and experience, employers should be able to determine more clearly those candidates that have performed well and will continue to do so in the classroom.

Using Evaluation Forms That You Have Built

When all candidates have been interviewed, how will you decide whom to hire? While every evaluation instrument has some subjectivity in it, an objective way to determine hires is to look at the total points or total number of target answers on a candidate's evaluation form and tally those numbers. For example, using the evaluation of candidate paperwork form from Chapter 3, there are 18 categories of criteria to be evaluated. One way to rank candidates is to total their number of target answers. A candidate with 16 targets would have a score of 16; one with 11 targets would have an 11. These numbers would then be added in to the number of target answers from the interview evaluation. The sample interview for a second-grade position has 15 questions that can receive a rating. Again, just count the targets for a sum.

Candidate A: 16 (from paperwork) + 10 (from interview) = score of 26

Candidate B: 11 (from paperwork) + 11 (from interview) = 22

Some evaluators will say that the interview is worth much more than the paperwork, so they will double the value of target answers from the interview.

Candidate A: 16 (paperwork) + 2 x 10 (interview) = 36

Candidate B: 11 (paperwork) + 2 x 11 (interview) = 33

Because weighted formulas can change the final outcome, the employer must decide on the final formula before using the evaluation forms. Another way to simplify the tallying is to rate the paperwork on fewer factors than the interview. The cover letter, resume, and letters may each have only two or three criteria, so that the paperwork totals can be a maximum of six to nine points. How the formula is weighted, and if it is weighted, adds to subjectivity of the system. If the interview is considered more important, then rate target answers more.

Some interviewers may want to give two points for every target answer and one for every acceptable, since "acceptable" is not a bad thing. Then a final formula might look like:

Candidate A: 16 (paperwork) + 2 x 10 (target) + 4 (acceptable) = 40

Candidate B: 11 (paperwork) + 2 x 11 (target) + 4 (acceptable) = 37

With all of the above three formulas, candidate A is still ahead. Candidate A had very strong paperwork, indicating strong writing skills, educational background, and strong letters of recommendation. Ten "target" answers in the interview of 15 questions make him or her hard to beat.

If the evaluation instrument uses numeric scales of 1 to 5, 1 to 7, or other, then simply add the numbers for a total. When the paperwork evaluation has 16 criteria, and the interview has 18 questions, and the scale is 1 to 5, some sample scores may look like:

Candidate A: 56 (paperwork) + 72 (interview) = 128

Candidate B: 48 (paperwork) + 66 (interview) = 114

Candidate C: 49 (paperwork) + 72 (interview) = 121

If the employer feels that the interview should count twice as much as initial paperwork, then the same candidates' scores would be:

Candidate A: 56 (paperwork) + 2 x 72 (interview) = 200

Candidate B: 48 (paperwork) + 2 x 66 (interview) = 180

Candidate C: 49 (paperwork) + 2 x 72 (interview) = 193

Candidate A is still hired with either formula for totaling the paper-work and interview scores. Of course, it can be argued that paper-work scores do not even have to be considered, since the paperwork earned the candidate the interview. If that is the case, just look at the interview score. It can also be argued that the interview ques-tions should be worth three times as much as paperwork scores, since everyone can get three letters of recommendation from someone. That is a workable formula, also, but it must be clear to all using the evaluation instruments and score totaling formulas what the proce-dure is from the beginning.

What if more than one interviewer rates candidates? How are mul-tiple scores handled? If multiple evaluations will be used, then the simplest path is to average the scores for a final score.

Candidate A: 200 + 210 + 187 = 597 ÷ 3 = 199

Candidate B: 180 + 178 + 200 = 558 ÷ 3 = 186

Candidate C: 193 + 185 + 165 = 543 ÷ 3 = 181

In this case, candidate A still leads the candidates, but candidate B has been helped and ranks second now, due to having three evalu-ators. When multiple evaluators are used, there can be a wide dis-crepancy among their scores. Some evaluators are simply looking for different answers. If an evaluator saw a candidate student teach, or knows them from a previous job, their score can be indicative of the past acquaintance (positive or negative) and not just the answers to interview questions.

One more way to use multiple evaluations is for each evaluator to rank their candidates, then to assign numbers to each ranking. A first choice earns a 5, second a 3, and third a 1. If there are more than three candidates, those below third receive no points. Let's look at how this can play out with an interview team of three evaluators and four candidates.

Evaluator one's ranking: Candidates A, C, B, and D

Evaluator two's ranking: Candidates C, A, D, B

Evaluator three's ranking: Candidates A, B, C, D

Evaluator four's ranking: Candidates C, A, B, D

Candidate A has earned the following points: 5 + 3 + 5 + 3 = 16

Candidate B has earned the following points: 1 + 0 + 3 + 1 = 5

Candidate C has earned the following points: 3 + 5 + 1 + 5 = 14

Candidate D has earned the following points: 0 + 1 + 0 + 0 = 1

Candidate A has earned the highest number of points and should be offered the job. Interestingly, the committee of four was divided on A and C for their top choice, but with one ranking of third for candidate C, candidate A was a clear top choice. Using a simple numeric can really shorten the time that a committee deliberates, and adds to the objectivity of hiring. Interviewers should stick with their original rankings and not have the opportunity to change rankings after they see their colleagues' final ranking. Committees that interview need fair, firm leaders. Once a committee decision is made, interviewers must also be professional enough to never tell a new hire that they were his or her second choice.

A Bottom Line of Quality

If a candidate is exceptionally strong, and does not have family ties to the community, he or she will probably be interviewing in multiple districts. Before calling the top candidate with a job offer, ranking the candidates and deciding how far down the list you can go to hire a well-qualified candidate is important. If you find that the first choice was unavailable, then knowing that you and/or a committee feel comfortable with one or even two more of the candidates will make your job easier. If a candidate is totally unacceptable, and the acceptable choices decline or accept jobs elsewhere, you are certainly not obligated to hire a weak candidate just because he or she interviewed for the position. Other options exist and include going back to the paperwork for more possible candidates, reopening and re-advertising the position, redefining a position, and taking the position to a wider audience through online, out-of-state, or out-of-country recruiting.

The idea of "casting a wider net" is being used by large school systems to fill positions. Hiring provisionally certified or non-fully certified candidates is an option in some states, but non-fully certified personnel may need support resources and training that are not available in your district, or that are expensive to implement. Be aware of union issues if non-fully certified personnel are hired when fully certified people were finalists for interviews.

What about "qualitative" evaluations and "feelings" about the candidate? If one individual makes a final decision, he or she may be genuinely torn between two strong candidates. Everyone in education knows stories of people who hire based on what they feel is "neediness" of a candidate for a job (single parent status or cut from another school due to budget), while others hire on the basis of coaching skills. The whole purpose of BBI is to hire candidates who are most likely to be able to succeed at the job, because of their past behaviors and experiences. Not only are there federal and union guidelines against discrimination in hiring, but hiring the best qualified person is the right thing to do for the sake of the students, the rest of the faculty, and the community. Every attempt should be made to make final decisions on the candidate's previous experience, behaviors, and expertise. The one qualitative question that does make sense is to ask yourself, "Would I want this candidate teaching my own child?"

Extending the Job Offer

How the job offer is extended, and the immediate follow-up are actually big factors in the new hire's decision to accept and remain in the position. New hires want to feel special and that they have "won" this job. A new hire once said that she felt as if she had won the lottery when the employer called to offer her a job. Every new hire should be excited. As one superintendent said, "If there is no flame of excitement at the beginning of a teaching career or new job, they can't burn out because they started with no flame. It's over already and I don't want any of our students in that teacher's classroom."

Compliment the candidate when the job offer is extended. Let them know that you and the faculty look forward to working with them.

Be clear about the specifics of the contract, and the time frame for getting a firm acceptance from the candidate. Common sense dictates that candidates give a tentative "yes" or "no," but be allowed some time to discuss the offer with parents or significant others. If a candidate is hesitant, and you really want him or her in the position, be encouraging and ask that they think about it and call you back or even come by to discuss further questions. Of course, have a timeline of your own. Candidates should not need more than two to three days to answer your offer with a yes or no.

Follow up the verbal answer with a letter of intent or contract. In this day and age, everyone has been taught to get promises "in writing." Be specific with potential new hires about when the letter or contract must be returned. If a letter is sent and not a contract, be sure that the letter states how the contract will be sent after school board approval. Warn candidates that failure to return a contract by a deadline negates it.

During the job offer phone call, explain to new hires what paperwork is due and the details of completing and returning it to the correct office. Since some candidates are very excited when they receive the call, it is always best to include written directions with the paperwork when it is sent.

End the call with heartfelt congratulations and let new hires know that they will be contacted about start dates for school and induction programs. One of the best ways to retain new hires is to follow up on all promises, keep them fully informed, and have the realities of the new positions meet or exceed their expectations. Job loyalty is built from day one, and the job offer itself is a step in building good employee relations.

The Value of Hiring Early

"In addition to the hiring process itself, the timing of hiring may af-fect new teachers' initial success and ensuing satisfaction. Specifically, relative to the school calendar, the date on which a teacher is hired may profoundly affect his or her chance of achieving positive results in the classroom. The stressors induced by late hiring, on top of the predict-able struggles inherent in learning to teach, may seriously threaten new teachers' satisfaction with their jobs and their intention to remain in the profession" (Johnson, et al., p. 32).

Hire as early as possible. New graduates want to be settled and ready for their first jobs, and new hires who are changing careers into teach-ing may have an even stronger need for their job to be decided so that they can then organize family matters. Start looking at the new school year's hiring needs as early as possible and work toward hiring well before the first new teacher orientation sessions begin. Late hires may feel that they were just afterthoughts, or that others were picked before them because of better skills. If late hires are made due to last minute enrollments or newly released money for personnel, always let the new hires know that the reasons were purely administrative and they are indeed valued faculty members.

"An unknown number of talented candidates may be lost every year due to an excessively long hiring process that occurs too late" (McCarthy & Guiney, 2004, p. 3).

Negotiations

The world of elementary, middle, and high school teaching is different from the business world, and from higher education. In teaching, there is little room for salary negotiation, since salaries are set by a district contract with the teachers' union and by state guidelines. Candidates should know the salary well before receiving the phone call that offers the position.

Some negotiation room may exist if a new hire wants to take on coaching duties or other extracurricular activities that carry salary stipends. Some candidates will begin to negotiate once the offer is extended for these duties. A candidate may be very abrupt and say, "I appreciate your offer, but I can't accept unless you can find coaching jobs that will add X thousand dollars to my base pay." At this point, you, as an employer need to be equally honest about these possibilities. Hopefully, the coaching and extracurricular activities were discussed during the interview and the offer includes duties that the candidate expects.

Teaching might be a little more attractive if it carried some of the perks of the business world, such as moving expenses, help with finding a job for a spouse, or even reimbursement for gas mileage to the interview. While these things are routine in business, they are generally not done for teachers. However, providing information about available housing and community services can be a very welcoming gesture. If the community offers "welcome wagon" type information or freebies, take advantage of those programs to help new teachers become established. (Of course, a few districts do provide incentives, such as free rent for six months in a nearby apartment complex or a signing bonus that can be used toward moving expenses, and these pluses help recruit teachers.)

What might new hires want to negotiate? Some new hires may want to negotiate their class schedule (more upper level than lower level classes), their classroom location, or even which students are omitted from their class roster (large numbers of special education or ESOL students). Again, these decisions should have been made by the school before the interview, and if enrollment patterns are unknown during hiring, it must be clear that the new teacher will have a fair mix of the new students and will be assigned a classroom as one becomes available. New hires shouldn't have to negotiate because these issues should be policy. Explaining policy during the interview and during the initial job offer should make expectations clear. If a candidate says that he or she cannot sign a contract until there is a guarantee of certain students, rooms, or assignments, then the employer has to say that those decisions cannot be made at this point and that the offer will be rescinded by a given date. Potential hires who can't handle limited uncertainty may not be the best candidates for the position. Again, be honest about what will happen and about unknown enrollments.

Have you ever heard of a new hire being given preferential treatment? Of course this can happen. Imagine for a moment how upset the returning faculty might be when it is discovered that the new hire received a classroom considered the "best" or hand-selected students. While some research indicates that new teachers experience more success when given fewer preparations and lighter teaching loads their first year, this has to be a school or districtwide policy to be enforced (and it would be a great idea). Without a policy in place, employers cannot give away the farm to make new hires happy without making veteran teachers unhappy, and possibly turning the faculty against the new hires before they even meet! Be fair and have a clear policy. Don't promise new hires something that can't be delivered just to get them to sign a contract.

Informing Faculty of New Hires and Stopping Gossip

Once contracts are signed, announce that positions are filled. If final room and class assignments are made with contracts, announce them as well. If final assignments are not available, do not announce tentative guesses and then change them. This is demoralizing to all involved.

Remind everyone involved in the hiring process that the discussions of candidates' rankings are confidential. It can be highly detrimental for a new hire to hear that he or she was not a first choice, or that two colleagues voted against him or her. Equally bad is a new hire who hears that everyone expected and wanted another candidate, or that he or she was chosen after a number of others said no to the job. It is difficult to stop gossip about new hires, but every effort should be made to keep administrative and faculty conversations about the subject professional. Working collaboratively with the union on a procedure to announce and welcome new hires may prove very beneficial. Once hired, continue to welcome and support the new teachers.

Chapter 9
Moving Forward to Induction and Mentoring

Hiring has become a yearlong process. Recruiters are offering contracts to strong candidates in February for August start dates. Year-round and balanced calendars mean that some districts are ending a school year in June and starting one in July, with a narrow window to hire new people if much work isn't done when classes are in session. January hires mean interviews take place during the fall semester and, of course, there are always unforeseen openings due to illness, family responsibilities, and early or unexpected retirements. The more policies and procedures that are in place to help new hires who join the school at anytime during the school year, the more supported those employees will feel.

Paperwork for Employment

Obviously there is a lot of paperwork to complete. Have one person make a checklist of paperwork that must be sent to, and received from, each candidate. The checklist may include:
- letter of intent,
- contract,
- tax forms,
- proof of citizenship/eligibility to work,
- insurance paperwork—including life insurance beneficiaries,

- criminal background check,
- emergency contact information,
- retirement account information, and
- proof of teacher certification/final transcripts after graduation.

Whenever possible, have new hires take care of everything before school starts, since the paperwork itself can be overwhelming. New hires need to concentrate on readying their classrooms and planning for instruction when they report for the school year.

Helping New Teachers Become Established in the Community

Aside from the mandatory paperwork, a welcome letter must be included. This letter can contain information about housing, health care, child care, businesses, churches, and community events. Many new teachers are new to the community as well, and need help finding services of all kinds. Being hired early, or at least before school starts, can be a significant factor in whether or not the new employee gets settled and established. Being settled and becoming a part of the community may be initial steps in retention.

Orientation Before School Starts

How new hires feel about the beginning of their career in your district sets the tone for whether or not they will remain. Because of this, orientation is crucial. As soon as candidates become new hires, alert them to orientation by inviting them to participate. Yes, orientation is mandatory, but an invitation is a nice touch. It is especially nice if the first part of orientation is a dinner sponsored by local merchants, or a breakfast or luncheon that is a little bit "upscale" in nature. As one superintendent said, "We want our new hires to feel that our district is not only supportive, but fun. We want them to bond and make friends so that they can have support from each other early on in the year."

Orientation for new hires should be held before the regular school orientation, since new hires need all of the information you will be sharing with veteran teachers, as well. If at all possible, pay the new hires a stipend for these workshops. Even fast-food workers are paid for their training, so shouldn't professional educators be treated as well? If stipends aren't possible, at least have great snacks, some free teaching supplies, and maybe a door prize.

Guidelines for Successful Orientation

1. All participants need to know the dates, times, and places as early as possible. While you are inviting them, they need to know that this is required and important. Let them know that the kick off brunch will be memorable, and the finale of orientation will be meeting a mentor who will have time to work with them one-on-one. Follow through with these promises.

2. A comfortable building environment will make or break any meeting. Add snacks, breaks, and materials, such as pens, paper, markers, etc.

3. Getting acquainted is important. It is best to help teachers get to know others in their subject and grade. Yes, they need to know who's who in the central office, but more importantly they need

to know someone who is nearby for a quick question before the first day of class.

4. Don't read material to teachers. Make the learning active. If you give a binder of information, ask them to pair up and then ask questions of the pairs about specifics in the binder. (Where do you call when you are sick? Who do you see to check on a payroll/insurance issue?) Award points for the teams and give a prize. It's active and they learn where to find the material in the binder.

5. Have other veteran teachers share experiences and "teach." The teachers will like this better than hearing from just one person. Of course, the presenting teachers will need specific topics and time limits. Consider having 2nd- or 3rd-year teachers present ideas; new hires can relate more easily to other fairly new teachers.

6. Ask the new teachers for input about what they want to know. Some may already know this district well, while others don't even know where the other schools are located. Use the teachers' input for content about the seminars and be sure to have teachers evaluate the orientation program.

Ongoing Support Seminars

The orientation meetings are just a beginning; good teacher induction should be ongoing throughout the first and second years of teaching. How does a school district make time for ongoing support seminars for new teachers? Many models already exist (see Breaux & Wong, 2003, for some examples). Some districts provide one after-school meeting a month for new hires throughout the year. Advertising the topics, they let teachers choose five of the offerings to earn district professional development credit. Many schools use professional development credit or graduate credit to lure teachers to after-school programs.

If at all possible, teachers should be given the opportunity to have support seminars during the school day. One district hired substitute teachers to allow for professional development seminars for their teachers. The new hires each received one half day per month to attend the seminars. Secondary teachers attended in the mornings because many coached in the afternoons and elementary teachers attended in the afternoons because they didn't want to miss their critical morning reading times with students (Clement, 2000).

What do new teachers want to discuss and learn about during these seminars? Ask them at the beginning of the year and they will tell you! (See Table 9.1). Also, using teacher input makes teachers more interested in attending. Many new teachers report that they want help with classroom management, students' social and emotional needs, teaching strategies, and stress management for themselves (Clement, 2000). Mostly, they need time to talk about the joys and concerns they are encountering in the classroom. They need to share and to feel that they are not alone when the classroom door closes.

A team of teachers or someone in the field of curriculum and instructional development can lead these seminars. Bring in unit experts in special education at some point in the school year. Having professors from a nearby university present and guide discussion is another way to build partnerships with the university. A hidden bonus in this is that colleges need to know what their graduates are experiencing during the first years so that they can better prepare candidates for teaching.

If some of the new hires are not yet certified teachers, their ongoing professional development must be the completion of their certification programs. Some districts are bringing courses on-site to help their non-fully certified teachers complete their training. Others are pairing with universities and regional offices of education to do this. In addition to formal classes for certification, make sure that these teachers receive some extra orientation about school law, classroom management, and student privacy issues. People who are brand new to teaching and who are taking their coursework concurrent to their first year(s) in the classroom tend to "teach as they were taught," and breaking this mold is very important. For example, a new hire that had yet to complete education courses said, "I figured when things got bad, I would yell and make examples of kids. If I embarrass them enough, they should be quiet." This is not best practice in management, but with no formal training, these kinds of attitudes exist.

Obviously, teachers who are still taking coursework need a very different type of support system than ones who completed a year of student teaching before joining the faculty. Teachers who are new to the district, but who have years of experience, need support, but not like the brand-new hires. When possible, individualize the support groups. One new teacher returned to her college campus at homecoming and told her professor, "I couldn't believe the orientation meetings. They taught us how to write a lesson plan. Can you believe it? And the scary part was that many of the new teachers acted like this was new information!" Getting to know the new hires and customizing their support can be a powerful method of providing help. Again, ask new hires what they want to see offered in seminars.

Table 9.1. Sample Seminar Topics Survey

Please take a moment and read the possible seminar topics for this year's new teacher program. Please rate the importance of each topic, using a scale of 1 to 3, where 1 indicates you feel the topic is unimportant, 2 indicates moderate importance, and 3 indicates that the topic is very important. The topics receiving the highest averages from the group will be scheduled for the meetings. Please circle your rating.

1. How to conduct a parent conference.   1 2 3
2. How to set up a grading scale/use the district grading policy.   1 2 3
3. How to work with the special education/inclusion teachers.   1 2 3
4. How to prepare students for the standardized state tests.   1 2 3
5. Curriculum—how to implement and cover the mandated topics.   1 2 3
6. Classroom management and discipline.   1 2 3
7. Stress management/time management for me.   1 2 3
8. Teaching strategies that motivate students and raise test scores.   1 2 3
9. How to prepare for my evaluations/portfolio/continued employment.   1 2 3
10. How to help students with social and emotional issues.   1 2 3
11. School law—what can and can't I do?   1 2 3
12. Violence prevention/conflict intervention.   1 2 3

Any other topic you would like to see?

What book do you recommend for every new teacher to read?

Mentoring

Mentoring has been in the world of education for decades—maybe centuries. New teachers often find a veteran teacher who can help them to "learn the ropes." Building a strong mentoring program can be compared to building a strong recruitment program—both take time, personnel, planning, and yes, a budget. The teacher's workday is very busy, and simply asking a teacher to make some time to help a new hire is not enough. Programs need to be planned and developed and mentors need training for their new roles. It has often been said that the skills needed to be a second-grade teacher and the skills needed to help someone else be a second-grade teacher are two different sets of skills.

Ganser states that a good mentoring program provides new teachers with "a more humane and professionally sound induction into teaching than a 'trial by fire' that serves neither teachers nor their students" (1999, p. 10). He also views the strong and lasting relationships that new teachers and their mentors often form as a "key feature in promoting the school as a learning community of professionals" (Gasner, 1999, p. 11; Educational Research Service, 2000)

Mentor Program Planning and Philosophy

Just how do mentor programs get started? A state may mandate mentoring, or the decision to implement a program may come from the superintendent. In some districts, the teachers' association/union assumes the responsibility for creating a mentoring program. A well-meaning teacher or administrator may start the program, or a team of teachers and administrators may do so. A university may offer its services to establish mentoring programs as a means of helping its graduates and soliciting feedback for program decisions.

No matter the origination of the program, the philosophy behind the mentoring program is critical. The administration and teachers need to agree on the philosophy before any planning is started. The biggest philosophical decision is the role of the mentor with regard to evaluation of the new hire, and the second decision is that of confidentiality. Mentors who do not report any evaluative data to administrators can encourage their protégés to open up about concerns and problems. Imagine the difficulty of getting a new teacher to talk about students throwing desks in a classroom if the new teacher knows that the mentor is one of his or her evaluators, or that the mentor can take any problems directly to the administration. Granted, some problems are so large that even a mentor must report them (child abuse, theft of school property), but confidentiality factors can create a program where new teachers don't hesitate to ask questions and get immediate help. Much has been written about establishing mentor programs (see, for example, Breaux & Wong, 2003; Scherer, 1999, 2003.)

Once the parameters of the program are established, mentors need to be selected and trained. A good mentor is a good teacher, but also someone who wants to spend time working with a new teacher. Many times mentors are teachers who have worked previously with student teachers or practicum students. One way to enlist mentors is to simply send a letter informing the teachers of the new program and to ask for applicants, using a short application/worksheet. Ask potential mentors if they have continued their own professional learning, and how. Ask if they have had experience "teaching" other teachers, in workshops or in their classrooms. Ask them why they want to mentor, looking for answers that indicate an interest in giving back to the profession. Who will screen the applications? A viable mentor program has a director, or someone who coordinates the mentor training and pairing of mentors with protégés. Again, an administrator or teacher may serve in this role. In one district, a teacher who was earning an administrative degree took on the project of developing a program for her required internship. She was also able to research the program for her next advanced degree.

What do mentors need to learn to be able to help their protégés? Mentors can gain much from learning how to observe their new teachers. The clinical supervision model of observation is a good one (Glickman, 2003) because it emphasizes collegiality. Mentors need awareness of how adults learn, since this may be the first time that they have taught other adults. Nothing hurts mentoring more than a mentor who just dictates! Mentors may need some listening and counseling skill training. Of course, it never hurts to ask new mentors to define what effective teaching is and watch the active discussion. Mentors may need help with finding resources for the new teachers. Role-playing of scenarios can be an important part of mentor training, since new mentors may not be aware of some of the types of concerns and questions they will encounter. Mentors may need follow-up training throughout the school year for their own support and well-being, since mentoring can prove stressful.

Another important aspect of training is that of helping mentors define their role. While they understand that their role includes answering questions and serving as a role model and guide, does it include teaching the new teacher how to do the math problems that will be taught the next day? Does mentoring mean that the mentor should loan money to a struggling new teacher with financial worries? Does it mean taking the new teacher out for coffee and an occasional dinner? Each district will set its own parameters, but even with established guidelines, mentors need to talk about possible questions and solutions from time to time. The most stressful part of mentoring may come in the early spring, when decisions about rehiring are made. A mentor may feel stress if his or her protégé is not rehired. The worst case scenario is if the new teacher decides to sue the mentor and the school district for not helping them achieve success. Yes, there is much to discuss in mentor training. (Clement, 2000).

Table 9.2. Mentor Training Topics

- The role of the mentor with regard to formal evaluation
- Confidentiality issues
- Awareness of adult learning
- How to observe in order to help (clinical supervision)
- Listening
- Counseling
- Helping with the nuts and bolts of instruction
- Classroom management
- Resources to share with new teachers
- Community resources

In addition to mentor training, the new hires need orientation about the role of their mentors. For example, some new teachers have been known to want to use their mentor as a paraprofessional, and when asked by the mentor if they need anything, the response is, "yes, please copy and staple my tests before next hour." A good orientation for new teachers includes what the mentors can and can not do for them.

Table 9.3. Practical Tips for Mentors
Make sure that mentors get practical tips for helping new teachers. For example: 1. Help the new teacher locate materials and supplies through sources other than their own money. 2. Make resource books and magazines available. 3. Share ideas for working with parents. 4. Share realistic classroom management plans. 5. Share strategies for teaching diverse student populations. 6. Update the new teacher on strategies that work. 7. Let the new teacher know it is okay to ask questions. 8. Model positive coping and stress relief strategies. 9. Invite the new teacher to become involved with a professional organization, but remind them that they can say "no" to requests to volunteer. 10. Listen, accept, and don't judge. (Clement, 1995, p. 40-41)

From Hiring to Retention

Just as BBI has come to education from the business world, so can ideas for retention. The most common ways to retain employees are to have strong salaries, good benefits, and a high quality workplace. Since salaries are usually determined by states, districts, and union negotiations, administrators need to work with state legislatures, local boards of education, and teachers' unions for the improvement of salaries. Benefits are improved the same way.

One way to retain teachers is to meet or exceed their expectations. Whatever was discussed (promised) in an interview must happen. Teachers who leave are those who say that the job was "not what they expected it to be." Being straightforward in interviews is the premise of BBI. After all, if past behavior is the best predictor of future performance, new hires should expect the employer's performance to match or exceed the behaviors they saw during the interview and the time between being hired and the first day of school. If teachers are told in orientation that they will receive help, then they must see that help materialize. If they are promised support with classroom management, that support must be consistent. These types of issues are important with regard to quality of the workplace. A lunch hour would be nice, too!

Retention will happen when new teachers are given realistic first assignments, meaningful professional development opportunities, and are treated as professionals. One way to provide a quality workplace is to simply listen to the teachers. They will express their needs and work towards improvements if they feel that they have a voice in decision making.

Improving the quality of the workplace is complicated. Some teachers say that the workplace would be better if it were cleaner, better cooled on hot days, and better heated on cold days. These problems can be fixed! Often teachers lament that they don't have offices or storage spaces. Again, administrators can work on space utilization, but only up to a point, since some schools are already bulging at the seams. Many teachers complain that they do not have what teachers in the best schools have, and it is difficult to make every school equivalent in supplies, resources, etc. However, when teachers really complain about the workplace, it is often in reference to things less tangible—respect, support, and professionalism.

As new teachers grow professionally, use their talents to serve on hiring committees, as mentors, and as trainers within the system. Not only do districts need to attract and keep new teachers, but they need to grow their own administrators as well. While it has been argued that teachers do not have a corporate ladder to climb, teachers can certainly ascend to being teacher leaders in their grade levels and building. Hire the best new teachers, support them, and watch them grow.

References

American Association for Employment in Education. (2000). *Recruiting the best.* Columbus, OH: Author.

American Association for Employment in Education. (2004). *Job search handbook for educators.* Columbus, OH: Author.

Beebe, B. (1996). The process called "behavior-based interviewing." *Journal of Career Planning and Employment, 56*(2), 40-47.

Breaux, A. L., & Wong, H. K. (2003). *New teacher induction: How to train, support, and retain new teachers.* Mountan View, CA: Harry K. Wong Publications.

Clement, M. C. (1995, September/October). If you really want to help the new teacher next door. *The Clearing House,* 40-41.

Clement, M. C. (2000). *Building the best faculty.* Scarecrow Press: Lanham, MD.

Clement, M. C. (2002). Help wanted: How to hire the best new teachers. *Principal Leadership, 3*(1), 16-21.

Clement, M. C. (2003). *The abc's of job-hunting for teachers.* Indianapolis, IN: Kappa Delta Pi.

Clement, M. C. (2004). Hiring the best middle school teachers with behavior-based interviewing. *Middle School Journal, 35*(4), 25-32.

Clement, M. C., Kistner, W., & Moran, W. (2005). Using behavior-based interviewing to hire the best new teachers. *Principal Leadership, 5*(9), 58-62.

Darling-Hammond, L. (2001). The challenge of staffing our schools. *Educational Leadership, 58*(8), 12-17.

Deems, R. S. (1994*). Interviewing: More than a gut feeling.* West Des Moines, IA: American Media Publishing.

Educational Research Service. (2000). *The informed educator series: Providing support for new teachers.* Arlington, VA: Author.

Futrell, M. H., Gomez, J., & Bedden, D. (2003). Teaching the children of a new America: The challenge of diversity. *Phi Delta Kappan, 84*(5), 381-385.

Ganser, T. (1999, October). Under their wings: Promises and pitfalls of mentoring. *The High School Magazine,* 10-13.

Gergen, D. (2005, July 11). Editorial: A teacher success story. *U. S. News and World Report, 139*(1), 78.

Glickman, C. D., Gordon S. P., & Ross-Gordon, J. M. (2003). *SuperVision and intructional leadership: A developmental approach* (6th ed.) Boston: Allyn and Bacon.

Gorman, D. (2000). On-campus recruitment more important than ever. *Recruiting the best.* Columbus, OH: American Association for Employment in Education.

Green, C. (1996). *Get hired! Winning strategies to ace the interview.* Austin, TX: Bard Press.

Haberman, M. (1995). *Star teachers of children in poverty.* West Lafayette, IN: Kappa Delta Pi.

Haggerty, D. (2001). Five steps to fire-proof your hiring process. *Business Credit, 103*(6), 12-13. Retrieved from Business Source Premier.

Head, S. (2000). Five steps to designing an effective teacher recruitment website. In D. Gorman, *Recruiting the best.* Columbus, OH: American Association for Employment in Education.

Heller, D. A. (2004). *Teachers wanted: Attracting and retaining good teachers.* Alexandria, VA: Association for Supervision and Curriculum Development.

Herrera, F. (2001). Demystifying hiring and retention. *Employment Relations Today, 28*(2), 87-95.

Ingersoll, R. M. (2003). The teacher shortage: Myth or reality? *Educational Horizons, 81*(3), 146-152.

Ingersoll, R. M., & Smith, T. M. (2003). The wrong solution to the teacher shortage. *Educational Leadership, 60*(8), 30-33.

Janz, T., Hellervik, L., & Gilmore, D. C. (1986). *Behavior description interviewing: New, accurate, cost effective.* Upper Saddle River, NJ: Prentice-Hall.

Johnson, S. M., Berg, J. H., & Donaldson, M. L. (2005). *Who stays in teaching and why: A review of the literature on teacher retention.* Boston: Harvard Graduate School of Education/The Project on the Next Generation of Teachers.

Kaplan, R. (2002). Handling illegal questions. *Planning Job Choices 2002.* Bethlehem, PA: National Association of Colleges and Employers.

Kistner, W. (1999, March). Past predicts future: Behavior-based interviewing. *Business to Business,* 16-17.

Liu, E. (2005, April). *Hiring, job satisfaction, and the fit between new teachers and their schools.* Paper prepared for the annual meeting of the American Educational Research Association, Montreal. Retrieved from www.gse. harvard.edu/~ngt.

McCarthy, M., & Guiney, E. (2004). *Building a professional teaching corps in Boston: Baseline study of new teachers in Boston's public schools.* Boston, MA: Boston Plan for Excellence.

McEwan, E. K. (2002). *10 traits of highly effective teachers.* Thousand Oaks, CA: Corwin Press.

McKenna, T. (2004). Behavior-based interviewing. *National Petroleum News, 96*(1), 16.

Naggy, E. (2002). Behavioral interviewing for educators. *2002 job search handbook for educators* (pp.20-21). Columbus, OH: American Association for Employment in Education.

National Commission on Teaching and America's Future. (1996). *What matters most: Teaching for America's future.* New York: Author.

Parkay, F. W., & Stanford, B. H. (1998). *Becoming a teacher* (4th ed.). Boston: Allyn and Bacon.

Parkay, F. W., & Stanford, B. H. (2004). *Becoming a teacher* (6th ed.). Boston: Allyn and Bacon.

Roling, T. & Vanderwall, L. (2000). Attending job fairs: Recruiting strategies for school employers. *Recruiting the best: A guide to successful recruitment strategies in education* (pp. 13-14). Columbus, OH: American Education for Employment in Education.

Scherer, M. (1999). A new teacher's world: Not your grandmother's classroom. In M. Scherer (Ed.), *A better beginning: Supporting and mentoring new teachers* (pp. vi-viii). Alexandria, VA: Association for Supervision and Curriculum Development.

Scherer, M. (ed.).(2003). *Keeping good teachers.* Alexandria, VA: Association for Supervision and Curriculum Development.

Steffy, B. E., Wolfe, M. P., Pasch, S. H., & Enz, B. J. (2000). *Life cycle of the career teacher.* Indianapolis, IN: Kappa Delta Pi.

Stronge, J. H. (2002). *Qualities of effective teachers.* Alexandria, VA: Association for Supervision and Curriculum Development.

Stronge, J. H., & Hindman, J. L. (2003). Hiring the best teachers. *Educational Leadership*, 60(8), 48-52.

The Teaching Commission. (2004). *Teaching at risk: A call to action.* Author.

Tye, B. B., & O'Brien, L. (2002). Why are experienced teachers leaving the profession? *Phi Delta Kappan*, 84(1), 24-32.

Voke, H. (2003). Responding to the teacher shortage. In M. Scherer (Ed.), *Keeping good teachers*. Alexandria, VA: Association for Supervision and Curriculum Development.

Willems, A. L., & Clifford, J. C. (1999). Characteristics of effective middle level teachers. *Education*, 119(4), 734-736.

Wiseman, D. L., Knight, S. L., & Cooner, D. D. (2002). *Becoming a teacher in a field-based setting* (2nd ed.). Belmont, CA: Wadsworth.

Wong, H. K., & Wong, R. T. (2004). *The first days of school: How to be an effective teacher* (3rd ed.). Mountain View, CA: Author.

Index

 # Subscriptions at a Glance

If you are looking for reliable preK-12 research to . . .

- tackle the challenges of NCLB;
- identify research-based teaching practices;
- make educationally sound and cost-effective decisions; and most importantly
- improve student achievement . . .

then look no further than an ERS Subscription.

Simply pick the subscription option that best meets your needs:

- ■ **School District Subscription**—a special research and information subscription that provides education leaders with timely research on priority issues in preK-12 education. All new ERS publications and periodicals, access to customized information services through the ERS special library, and 50 percent discounts on additional ERS resources are included in this subscription for one annual fee. This subscription also provides the entire administrative staff "instant" online, searchable access to the wide variety of ERS resources. You'll gain access to the ERS electronic library of more than 1,600 educational research-based documents, as well as additional content uploaded throughout the year.

- ■ **Individual Subscription**—designed primarily for school administrators, staff, and school board members who want to receive a personal copy of new ERS studies, reports, and/or periodicals published and special discounts on other resources purchased.

- ■ **Other Education Agency Subscription**—available for state associations, libraries, departments of education, service centers, and other organizations needing access to quality research and information resources and services.

Your ERS Subscription benefits begin as soon as your order is received and continue for 12 months. For more detailed subscription information and pricing, contact ERS toll free at 800-791-9308, by email at ers@ers.org, or visit us online at www.ers.org!

ERS ORDER FORM FOR RELATED RESOURCES

Quantity	Item Number	Title	Base Price	ERS Individual Subscriber Discount Price	ERS School District Subscriber Discount Price	Total Price
				Price per Item		
	0407	Essentials for Principals: How to Interview, Hire, and Retain High-Quality New Teachers	$25.95	$19.46	$12.98	
single copy only	5365	Info-File: Recruiting and Hiring Teachers	$40	$30	$20	
	0372	The Informed Educator: Providing Support for New Teachers	$9.60	$7.20	$4.80	
	0537	Concerns in Education: Teacher Compensation and Teacher Quality	$36	$27	$18	
		Shipping and Handling** (Add the greater of $4.50 or 10% of purchase price.)				
		Express Delivery** (Add $20 for second-business-day service.)				
**Please double for international orders.					TOTAL PRICE:	

SATISFACTION GUARANTEED! If you are not satisfied with an ERS resource, return it in its original condition within 30 days of receipt and we will give you a full refund.

Visit us online at www.ers.org for a complete listing of resources!

Method of payment:

☐ Check enclosed (payable to ERS)   ☐ P.O. enclosed (Purchase order #_____)

☐ MasterCard   ☐ VISA   ☐ American Express

Name on Card: _____ Credit Card #:_____

Expiration Date: _____ Signature: _____

Ship to: (please print or type) ☐ Dr.   ☐ Mr.   ☐ Mrs.   ☐ Ms.

Name: _____ Position: _____

School District or Agency: _____ ERS Subscriber ID#: _____

Street Address: _____

City, State, Zip: _____

Telephone: _____ Fax: _____

Email: _____

Return completed order form to:
Educational Research Service • 1001 North Fairfax Street, Suite 500 • Alexandria, VA 22314-1587
Phone: 703-243-2100 • Toll Free Phone: 800-791-9308 • Fax: 703-243-1985 • Toll Free Fax: 800-791-9309
Email: ers@ers.org • Web site: www.ers.org

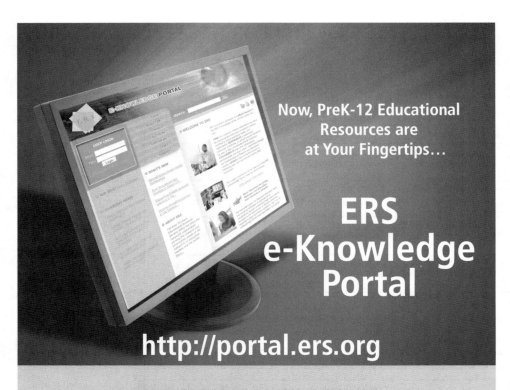